ISBN 978-0-9561103-0-5

Photographs are by the authors unless otherwise stated.

Design by Dale Wallace.
Printed in Ireland by FXPress Ltd., Ennis, Co. Clare.

10 Years On

Celebrating Ten Years of the
Limerick Garden Plants Group

Edited by J.Dennison and J.Baker

Introduction

The Limerick Garden Plants Group is celebrating ten years of activity, promoting, educating, and entertaining the people of Limerick with horticultural and gardening advice. Prior to our existence there was little that fostered gardening interest apart from a number of flower clubs, essentially dealing with flower arranging. Limerick, for a good number of years, was, horticulturaly speaking, according to its Viking name, a 'barren place'; although in the early 19th century, the 'Hanging Gardens of Limerick' William Roche's unique interpretation of the vertical garden, were so renowned as to bring visitors from afar to view them. The last ten years however, have seen a new flowering and a flourishing of interest in matters horticultural - in no small measure, due to the activities of the LGPG.

In 1998 a small number of people interested in forming the group, met in Nell Allott's house in Ballingarry, Co. Limerick, to discuss what the purpose and value of such an association would be; and to ascertain whether or not there would be sufficient interest amongst the wider public. Our uncertainty was quickly answered when we launched the Limerick Garden Plants Group later in the year. The membership rapidly rose to over one hundred or so, where it has hovered ever since. The reason for such a healthy figure, particularly now - when I hear of gardening groups all over the country either struggling to attract members or closing down - is without doubt due to the energy, commitment and dedication of a small group of people who form the LGPG committee and who in large part were the original group who met in Ballingarry. I congratulate them all for their achievements on this special occasion and offer them a huge thank you for their sterling work over the period.

On this, our tenth anniversary, we decided that to mark the occasion we would produce a publication made up of articles from some of our visiting speakers over the decade. Some of the articles are written specifically for this book; either based on their lectures to us or on some other topic. Others are reproduced with the author's permission, from other earlier publications. To them all, I would like to offer a very sincere word of thanks. All were asked to meet impossibly tight deadlines and their responses were most generous.

A very special thank you must also go to former Limerick man Dr. Peter Wyse Jackson, the Director of the National Botanic Gardens in Glasnevin, for very kindly agreeing not only to provide us with an article but also agreeing to write the foreword to the book.

Last but not least I would like to thank all those people and organisations who agreed to sponsor the publication of the book. Whether their contribution was small or large, it is most gratefully received. Without their help this archival record of the first ten years of the Limerick Garden Plants Group would not have happened.

Jim Dennison
Honorary Chairman
Limerick Garden Plants Group
September 2008

Foreword

It was a pleasure and honour for me to be asked to contribute a foreword for this valuable book, celebrating the 10th anniversary of the Limerick Garden Plants Group. A couple of years ago I was invited to speak at a meeting of the Group, very shortly after I had been appointed as director of the National Botanic Gardens in Glasnevin. Returning to Limerick was a joy for me not only because of the old friends I met there and new friends made but also because I spent my childhood in the city and it is where I first gained an interest in plants, gardens and the natural world.

Of course while I was growing up in the city, groups like the Limerick Garden Plants Group celebrating and promoting gardening, gardens and plants, did not exist. And in those days gardening did not have the huge following that it now enjoys in Ireland as probably our most important leisure pastime.

Even though the Group has only been established for ten years it has already become an important organisation supporting plants and gardens in the region. I know that its activities have been diverse, including regular lectures, some of them published as articles in this book; workshops when horticultural experiences and expertise can be passed on to others, and regular study visits to different gardens. The Group has not restricted itself just to gardens though and I know that regular excursions are made to one of Ireland's richest botanical areas, the Burren, to study the remarkable range of native Arctic-Alpine and Mediterranean plants that thrive there. One of the most important roles of the Group has been the preparation of publications such as this book, as well as its annual journal. Such publications ensure that the Group provides a valuable forum for exchange of information and news between members but also leaves a long-term legacy of important information on gardens and gardening in the 21st century that can be enjoyed and learnt from in the years to come.

The changing face of horticulture in these islands has meant that many plants and varieties that were formerly grown in gardens have become rare, and in some instances, close to extinction. The important role played by members of the Group in cultivating such plants, particularly Irish-bred varieties, is a valuable contribution to efforts to conserve our heritage of Irish horticultural plants. The expected impacts of climate change in Ireland over the coming century will make our gardening challenges even more pressing and threaten to change so much of the basis of our current gardening practices, including many of the plants we can grow. Groups such as the Limerick Garden Plants Group will be at the vanguard of finding ways to mitigate these changes, helping to ensure that not only are important plants maintained in our collections but also helping to find ways to ensure that gardening in Ireland remains sustainable and environmentally-friendly.

I was pleased to learn that like so many bodies today, the Group adopted a mission statement – to educate, inform and to extend knowledge and experience of gardening horticulture in the Mid-West. Being clear about its role and mission is essential if the Group is to be clear about its potential and what it wants to achieve. It is always useful to know where one is going before setting out on a journey! The Limerick Garden Plants Group clearly knows where it is going and I have no doubt that it will thrive and flourish in the years ahead and go on to many more successes in the future.

Congratulations on achieving this important 10th anniversary and best wishes for the next ten years and beyond!

Peter Wyse Jackson
National Botanic Gardens, Glasnevin
27th September, 2008

Content

A Decade of Gardening
by Ciaran Burke

L ooking back ten years; how short it seems and how much has changed. Gardens have got smaller, the weather drier, the climate has got warmer, vegetables have made a comeback, and gardeners have became consumers. Gardening is now a 'lifestyle'. It is everywhere, in newspapers, magazines, lifestyle glossies, radio programmes, local papers, satellite television, if not yet on Irish television.

I buck the trend of smaller gardens. Ten years ago I lived in a terraced house in Dublin with a small garden and quickly ran out of space and things to do. Now I live in a cottage with a one acre garden in Co. Mayo, and usually we have too much to do. On a personal level my garden has got bigger.

My climate change has been different. Having moved from east coast to west of Ireland I see a lot more rain and feel a lot more wind. The constant talk of English television presenters about saving water and the need to grow drought resistant plants seems like another world. Why is garden media coverage so much biased to the south of England? Not to trivialise the problem of water shortages, it is serious in many areas, but to talk of drought tolerant plants for the west of Ireland! Rarely while living in Dublin did I experience hard frosts, and rarer still, snow that lasted longer than one hour. Now I live in a valley which acts as a frost pocket. Every year we have had frosts and experience falls of snow that lingers for days.

My gardening has changed much over the past decade; civilised south county Dublin has been exchanged for the wilds of Mayo. We live on Askey road, meaning quagmire. Makes sense to us. The topography of the site includes changes in level and the lower parts, furthest from the house, are very wet. At the end of the garden runs a stream and beyond that there is bog. *Metasequoia glyptostroboides* and *Taxodium distichum* are settling in nicely. Part of our garden is on a gravel hill which provides perfect drainage. This is a blessing given our high rainfall. It allows us to grow plants that would otherwise rot in the ground. *Beschoneria yuccioides* which moved with me from Dublin took a while to settle in, but once it realised it was not going back, it stopped feigning sickness and now looks the picture of health. Alpines grow well in the stone mulched front garden, only because of perfect drainage. Around our house are large spruce trees which add maturity to the garden, provide some shelter, and create dry woodland conditions. In the dryness, *Myosotidium hortensia* grows happily alongside Hostas: an easy way of reducing slug damage. The contrasting conditions present opportunities to grow very different types of plants. We can make equal use of Beth Chatto's books: 'The Dry Garden', 'The Damp Garden' or 'The Woodland Garden'. It is great to have space.

In general, winters have got milder. While I was a student in the National Botanic Gardens in 1990, a plant of *Ficus pumila* growing at the entrance to the alpine yard was covered each October with Yew branches, to protect the plant from frost. Nowadays when I visit the gardens with groups of my students it is never covered and the plant is untouched by the icy fingers of Jack Frost. Plants which we might not have tried in our gardens ten years ago are thriving. At home we have grown *Pseudopanax lessonii* 'Goldsplash', *P. arboreus* and *P. laetus* for the last couple of years and despite what we would call cold winters, they have come through with little damage and are growing well.

I think that our ideas of hardiness have to be re-examined. Much of the information in books is based on writings from long ago. In many cases the main source of reference is still W.J. Beans: 'Trees and Shrubs Hardy in the British Isles'. While the species described have changed little since the first two volumes of this great four volume work were first published in 1914, the weather has. Bean states that most Cistus are not hardy outside. His observations are based on growing conditions of over 100 years ago and on the wisdom of previous generations in the 19th century. Now in the 21st century we experience little frost in comparison. The range of plants possible to grow on our Gulf Stream enhanced isle is wider than ever.

Gardening has become more popular. Every town has a garden centre, and lately DIY stores have jumped on the bandwagon. Paradoxically, as the garden retail outlets get bigger and more numerous, the range of plants seems to get smaller. Gardeners have been transformed into consumers, categorized by income and age group. In the minds of the marketing professionals the younger, richer, impatient consumer does not want to dig and weed, they want lifestyle accessories: patio heaters, stylish garden furniture, glazed pots, candles and specimen pot plants. I cannot believe this is true. Our courses are filled with enthusiastic gardeners unafraid to get their hands dirty.

Smaller gardens mean less space, which means fewer trees and shrubs are sold and planted. As more people look for smaller plants, retailers respond. Hebes dominate the plant displays, uniform growth habits and tidy domes of evergreen form a blanket of marketable foliage over the benches in the garden centres. Plants are judged by their shelf life and saleability, not by their beauty and garden performance.

Due to the paucity of the plant range offered, the gardeners have been yearning for good garden plants. In response, the last decade has seen a number of specialist nurseries emerge. Such establishments are usually run by plant enthusiasts who love the plants that they sell and grow. I am grateful to these plantaholics whose lives need more than just financial reward and who often go to great lengths to find, propagate and grow plants of interest. A keen gardener will drive miles to visit a good nursery.

A positive development over the last decade is the slow awakening of our environmental consciousness. Although there is still a long way to go, we are starting to consider the consequences of our garden activities. A new term has emerged in garden conversation: sustainability.

Attitudes within the horticultural industry are changing too. The use of chemicals to control pests is reducing. Matters such as peat extraction, the use of plastic pots, the environmental impact of MYPEX® and water conservation are being discussed seriously. Research is being conducted, alternatives being sought and action being taken. We all have a responsibility to take care of our environment and gardeners can lead the way.

Ten years may seem like a long time looking forward, but in the greater scheme of things it is but a moment. Trees can live hundreds if not thousands of years. Our gardening can be a legacy. What remains after we are gone is up to us.

A Foot, a Fork and a Garden

by Deborah Begley

Yes, that was an incredible time, 1998. So many doors in my life opened up that fateful year and, rather than choosing just one, I ran headlong through them all. I was there at the birth of the Limerick Garden Plants Group and ten years on it has lived up to all the promise it showed when seven of us got together and planned how to get it going. That year my husband Martin and I tentatively opened our young garden to the paying public. How we cringe now when we recall how raw it all was. We decided to call it Terra Nova, and so it followed that when I decided to launch my nursery later that year I called it Terra Nova Plants. In the intervening years we have welcomed thousands of people to our garden and said farewell to thousands of plants, all destined for a life (and death!) in gardens throughout Ireland. Some were considered to be so special that they found themselves heading for places such as Norway, Sweden, Germany, Japan and even the Dominican Republic. Lucky them!

But where would any gardener be without a driving force, a passion that transcends all the back breaking work, the wind, the rain and the occasional garden fork pushed through the foot. And in case you are wondering, yes it did hurt! Looking back in my records I see that it was 1998 when I first met with the two words that would steer me on a course of wonder and amazement, a path that led me straight to the fascinating world of aroids. *Dracunculus vulgaris.* As a child, I had braved many hours of self-inflicted, delicious terror, watching vampire movies, so I knew instantly that a plant bearing this evocative name would have

Dracunculus vulgaris

to be investigated further. When the pages of the *RHS A-Z Encyclopaedia of Garden Plants* fell open, my eyes were met with the sight of a lurid, yet strangely attractive-looking maroon coloured 'flower', a thing that looked as if it may have originated in outer space. It was love at first sight! Although it is very peculiar looking, *Dracunculus vulgaris* is a plant that most gardeners would enjoy growing. From the Mediterranean, it is very hardy and makes an early start into growth, shoving pointy snouts up through chilly January soil. By April it has reached a height of 1.5 metres. Mottled stems topped with ornate leaves become home to massive dark purple spathes in June. These smell horribly for about 24 hours, so need to be planted well away from the house! Summer dormant, it collapses into a messy heap by mid July. This is a plant with personality! So it stood to reason that other family members would be equally as mad and I made it my business to make their acquaintance asap. As Deni Bown writes in '*Aroids Plants of the Arum Family*', "Aroids are not the sort of plants you can be neutral about." On research, each type seems curiouser and curiouser. Although aroids (members of the botanical family *Araceae*) vary greatly in appearance, they all share the common hallmark of having a spathe and spadix inflorescence. The spadix is a poker-like protrusion, with clusters of tiny flowers, usually nestling at its base, whilst the spathe, a modified leaf, wraps itself around the spadix, with each genus taking on many bizarre guises, all managing to look as if they were dressing up for a Halloween party.

Arisaemas are my favourite of all aroids. Ten years ago they were only grown by a handful of plant geeks, but in the past few years they have become one of my best selling plants. Hail the Arisaema! Herbaceous plants growing from a tuber, the Indian, Chinese, Japanese and American species are all hardy enough to be grown outside in an Irish garden and although they are mainly woodland plants, best placed in dappled shade, they will survive in a more open situation. *Arisaema tortuosum* is such a variable species and as I grow lots of them from seed from different sources, I now have a good collection. A robust plant, eventually reaching over a metre tall, the spathes are often green and the long upward pointing spadices either green or dark purple. Some forms have beautiful mottling on the stems. One of my favourite Arisaemas is *A. dilatatum*, a big plant in all senses of the word. Huge rough trifoliate leaves surround purple-flecked green spathes with spadices reminiscent of green elephant trunks. *A. candidissimum* is a very popular plant and considerably 'prettier' than other species. So pretty in fact that it was chosen to adorn the front cover of this very book! The pink and white

Arisaema dilatatum

striped spathes appear very late in the season and the mid-June emergence worries most gardeners who fear that it may be lost. It never is! The dinky little *A. kiushianum* is in a pot in my working greenhouse, not because it's tender, but because I want to enjoy the chirpy little owl faced thing at close quarters. It is difficult to leave this section without mentioning the May flowering *A. sikokianum*. This Japanese species is a showstopper; the black spathe has a pure white interior that is home to a dumpy club-shaped white spadix. Desired by everybody, this is a nurseryman's dream plant as it is notoriously short lived. But there's something very peculiar about *Arisaema sikokianum*, and I'm not just talking about its appearance. I know that it may not be scientifically possible, but I'd swear that this plant has a sense of humour. Some years back, an American grower reported strange occurrences in his colony. Planted in an open situation on one side of a pathway, every bloom came up with its shiny black back facing the path. Thinking it was a reaction to the sun, he lifted them whilst in flower (you can do this with these plants!) and planted them on the other side of the path, facing the astonishing white spathes inwards. The following year, up they came again, every one of them with their back turned to the path! I laughed

when I read it, but lately it's been happening to me too...

Affectionately known as the 'poor cousin' of Arisaema, Pinellia's may be less well-known, but they are very quirky, so that buys them a free pass to enter my garden. They are easily grown, in fact some gardeners might say *too* easily grown, although that is not a problem here. There are six species, all Asian, the most well-known being *P. ternata*, nicknamed 'the little green dragon' because of its slender green spathes and long, upward pointing spadices. This trifoliate species has the unusual habit of producing bulbils in the base of the stalks, these drop to the ground and under the right circumstances form large colonies. Along with this I also grow *P. pedatisecta* which has much divided leaves and a long yellowish-green spathe with a concealed spadix. A favourite plant is the purple form of the normally green flowered *Pinellia tripartita*. The attractive

Arum italicum 'Mamoratum'

leaves are divided into three parts and the inflorescence sits proudly above these displaying a very long, slender antenna-like spadix. The 'mouse plant' *Arisarum proboscideum*, native to Italy and Spain, forms dense colonies of low-growing, dark green sagittate leaves. The 'mouse' part of their common name refers to the inflorescences that appear among the foliage in May. The plant produces an abundance of dumpy little brown and white spathes that have remarkably long whip-like tips, giving them the appearance of a nest of tiny mice diving for cover beneath the leaves. Pollinated by fungus gnats, the concealed spongy white spadix emits a faint mushroomy aroma to lure them in. Happy in my heavy clay, this charming little plant being summer dormant dies back to a cluster of very small rhizomes in July.

There are 25 species of Arum, a genus of tuberous perennials occurring from the Azores to western China and from Sweden to Morocco. Our own native *A. maculatum*, the familiar 'lords and ladies' of our hedgerows doesn't really makes its presence felt until it bears drumsticks of bright red berries in the early autumn. From one seed head of an open pollinated group, this variable species is capable of producing many apparently different offspring. Some may have the classic plain, deep green leaves; whilst the foliage of others may be heavily spotted with black, a highly desirable trait to the arum collector. The spathes also vary greatly in both size and colour, coming in shades of pale greenish-white or yellow or dull pink or purple. A wild seedling in my own garden exhibits a strong purple flush, much to my pleasing. There is a yellow variegated form of *A. maculatum* named 'Painted Lady' that grows very weakly here, barely surviving from year to year, a problem encountered by most growers. The deservedly well-known garden plant, *Arum italicum* subsp *italicum* 'Mamoratum' grows here with wild abandon, the birds doing an "excellent" job of distributing the ripe seeds to every section of the garden. The handsome silver-veined foliage of this plant appears in early winter and the urine-scented greenish-white flowers arrive in April/May. These have produced some very striking progeny, and I now have colonies of plants that bear varying degrees of silver markings, including some with solid silver-centred leaves. I also grow other excellent named forms, *A.* 'Chameleon', with its very attractive grey/ green marbled leaves, and the creamy-yellow variegated *A.italicum* subsp.*neglectum* 'Miss Janay Hall'. *Arum concinnatum* looks remarkably like *A. italicum* subsp. *neglectum* 'Mamoratum' and is just as easy to grow. It is reputedly slightly tender, but mine survives quite happily under the canopy of a clump of Gunnera.

Early April is an exciting time in the Arum calendar, as the highly desirable *Arum creticum* starts to unfurl stands of long, spiky pale yellow buds. On opening, the spathes turn back on themselves, creating the enchanting 'turk's cap' effect. The much protruding, beaky, deep yellow spadix makes the sight even more memorable. If *A. creticum* is 'the beauty' then *A. dioscoridis* and all of its forms and varieties surely qualify as 'the beast'. Easy to grow, these spectacular plants produce the strongest smell, described as a mix of dung

Arum berries

and rotting meat, of the entire Arum family. Big green inflorescences, heavily blotched in darkest purple are produced alongside the dark green leaves in April. Among other Arums lurking here at Terra Nova, is *A. pictum*, the only autumn-flowering species. This produces dark purple, sail-like spathes, which emerge alongside the attractively veined, glossy leaves. It is grown in a warm spot in the garden, as its hardiness is not guaranteed. It also grows well in pots kept under glass.

I find *Alocasia macrorrhiza*, the giant taro, highly desirable. It is used as a food source in the tropics but is distinctly tender here. The growth in summer is amazing, the dramatic, giant glossy leaves working brilliantly in my exotic border, but in the past I have forgotten to dig it up and overwinter under glass, so have lost it more than once. A newly acquired plant from Homebase is safely planted into the border of one of my greenhouses and I am full of hope that we shall see in many years together.

I've had some success with a small handful of the 200 species of Amorphophallus. Most of these are tender plants, but *A. konjac* is reliably hardy, surviving winter temperatures as low as -10°C. This plant is a real talking piece. In early June the tuber produces a tall, solitary, green and white mottled leaf stalk that is topped by a much-dissected parasol of leaflets. A young tuber will only produce this leaf, but once mature it becomes capable of producing a bloom. Flowering has only occurred here twice in the past seven years, with the slugs making shreds of the maroon coloured spathes. Maybe they are attracted by the foetid smell. As most Amorphophallus tubers have a horrible tendency to rot, they are best kept bone dry in their dormant season. Once I was the proud owner of a football-sized tuber of the outrageously bizarre *A. paeoniifolius*, but alas it was potted up too soon, watered before it had started into strong growth and rot set in. Despite major surgery on the tuber and the application of copious amounts of green sulphur nothing would halt the march of decay. Very sad.

The 'voodoo lily', *Sauromatum venosum'* is an amazing and grotesquely amusing plant. Capable of producing a foul-smelling 30cm tall flower on a naked corm, this plant is great fun to share with children! It makes a good garden plant, totally hardy here for over 10 years now. The inflorescence is followed by a 50cm tall, single, green and brown mottled stem, which is topped with an interesting arrangement of dissected leaves. Good in the open ground, even better in a pot. This is rapidly becoming the top selling plant in my nursery.

So diverse is the great family of aroids that whilst some of them will rapidly rot if given too much water, others absolutely revel in it.

Orontium aquaticum is an aquatic aroid from North American. It's a strange
looking thing as its spathes are invisible under the water level, leaving loads
of slender, yellow-tipped white spadices poking up out of the water; these
are joined by long glaucous leaves. It is grown in a basket that is submerged
30cm under water and is slow to bulk up. 'Skunk Cabbages' also like wet
conditions. I grow the Asian species, *Lysichiton camtschatcensis* in a large basket
on the ledge of a pond. It produces robust, pure white spathes and big greeny-
yellow club-like spadices that are followed by huge glossy, ovate-oblong leaves.
The larger, yellow flowered American species *Lysichiton americanus* is capable
of forming huge colonies in boggy ground, as can be witnessed at Annsgrove
Garden, Castletownroche, Co. Cork. In our garden the plant is restricted to a
pot submerged in the wildlife pond. *Zantedeschia aethiopica* is a good marginal
plant. I have some lovely pink flushed forms, 'Glow' and 'Marshmallow Pink',
they are utterly divine and very well named. *Zantedeschia aethiopica* 'Pershore
Fantasia' has green and yellow variegated leaves, but division of this plant tends
to produce lots of reversion to plain green. Z. 'Green Goddess, is a lovely
plant, its white spathes so heavily flushed with green as to almost obliterate
the whiteness. A few years ago I raised a batch of plants from seeds named *Z.
aethiopica* 'white speckled form'. These have grown into attractive plants, the
leaves sprinkled with a generosity of white spots and the spathes green tipped.

Any of the aroids that I have grown from seed take at least three years to
produce a bloom, some considerably longer, with *Symplocarpus foetidus*, taking
the biscuit. I sowed fifty fresh seeds in October 1999. In October of 2002
the potful of seeds that had been inspected what seemed like a trillion times,
finally produced forty two seedlings. To some this may seem like a ridiculous
amount of time to wait, but due to the huge, deep questing rootstocks that
this plant has, it's really the only feasible way to propagate it. From boggy areas
of Northeast America, this is one of nature's wonders. Flowering early in the
year, the owl-shaped spathes are able to push themselves up through frozen
ground thanks to the little 'horn' on each head and to the heat generating

spadix within. How brilliant is that? Six years have passed since those little sprouts appeared; most have winged their way in parcels across the world, including rather ironically New York State, a home of *Symplocarpus foetidus*. Understandably, due to the extensive nurturing involved, I became rather attached to those plants and often wonder how they are getting along! As for my own specimens, I am still patiently waiting to for them to flower; hopefully they will do it sometime before I start drawing my pension.

So, my passion for aroids is obvious, but not everybody is as smitten. A friend stood looking at an Arisaema in flower. He looked puzzled for a few moments, then turned to me and said "But what's the point of it?" Over the years I have been amused to note other people's feelings on their first encounter with the more unusual aroids. Some stare in wonderment at nature's fantastical creation, whilst others ask, "What will it look like when it comes into flower?"

A Snowdrop and Hellebore Extravaganza

by Tim Ingram

Winter turning into spring is one of the most evocative and wonderful times in the garden. Some of the earliest flowers are the hellebores which begin to grow through milder spells in the height of winter, and can be had in flower from December right through to April, or even May. These are plants of great substance and character in the garden, ultimately forming strong and long-lived clumps if cared for. They are fascinating to collect, with a growing diversity of flower colours and forms: black, white, green, yellow, red, doubles, picotees, spotted within, or with coloured nectarines. Though many gardeners prefer types that hold their flowers up and show the markings within, their more natural nodding habit is well designed to protect them from harsh weather. Like the snowdrops that grow with them, there is great delight in stooping to hold the flowers up and study them closely. A famous French gardener is said to use an angled mirror on a walking stick specifically to enjoy the markings of hellebores in the winter garden.

'Snowdrops' courtesy of Jenny Baker

The enthusiast will also become drawn to some of the less common species of hellebores such as *H. viridis*, a rare British native, which can have almost glowing green flowers set against much deeper green foliage. In the dry south-east *H. multifidis* which grows in the hotter and drier climes of the Balkans, can make a spectacular foliage plant; its leaves cut into innumerable narrow leaflets almost like a miniature palm. This too has small green flowers very early in the year, which for me, sadly, are often devoured by mice for their sweet nectar before they set any seed. One of the loveliest of all, though usually too tender for most gardens, is the Majorcan *H. lividus*, effectively a small and more colourful form of the Corsican hellebore *H. argutifolius*. It can have beautifully silver-marbled leaves, like cyclamen and extraordinary flowers of purplish-pink without and apple-green within. I grow it in a gritty loam in deep pots, kept on a sunny patio except in the cold depths of winter.

Hybrids of this and its relatives with the Christmas Rose, *H. niger*, are hardy plants of great class and vigour, well worth acquiring though slow to produce and quite expensive. All of this group are best in a warm, fairly sunny and well drained spot which gets quite dry in summer.

'Snowdrops' courtesy of Deborah Begley

Snowdrops go with hellebores like fine wine with a meal and can command similar prices. Their pristine white bells with subtle but ever so interesting markings are the epitome of winter. Why should they hold us so much in their thrall? It must be their simplicity and purity in the often harsh days of the new year. Remarkably quickly one can move from admiring wide drifts of

the native *Galathus nivallis* in country churchyards, to conversing deeply about
the merits of 'Merlin' over 'Magnet' or whether 'Chadwick's Cream' goes with
'Blueberry Tart'. My favourite combination could well be 'Big Boy' walking out
with 'Long Tall Sally'! It is not only the flowers of snowdrops that are valuable
in the garden; their leaves can be very striking too. In *G. plicatus* and *T. elwesii*
they are broad and long and often coloured silvery-grey or blue green. On the
bank next to the rock garden at the Royal Horticultural Society Garden at
Wisley, these make superb ground cover under big tall oaks, mixed with crocus,
cyclamen, hellebores and other winter flowers. At the other extreme, the petite
G. gracilis has thin twisted leaves and makes a pretty addition to a small alpine
trough or raised bed. Some snowdrops, like *G. woronowii* from southern Russia
and north-east Turkey, have green glossy leaves quite at odds with most of their
relatives. All in all they are entirely captivating in the garden.

  With the snowdrops and hellebores rise a harmony of other winter and
early spring flowers. In open and sunny places, small bulbs, crocus, iris, ipheion,
muscari and narcissus come to the fore. Some will grow quite happily in grass
where they can look particularly well suited. Others, needing a more gritty
well drained spot, will do well with small sun-loving perennials and alpines.
The crocus is especially alluring with different species flowering from autumn
through to spring. I have many in a round bed in the middle of the lawn
where they are less susceptible to the burrowings of mice and other pests.
Very keen growers keep them in a cold greenhouse where their beautiful
chalice-like flowers will not be shattered by the often blustery winter weather.
Their leaves and flowers unfortunately are like caviar to rabbits, but some
are left alone including the beautiful mid-winter flowering *C. laevigatus*
'Fontenayi', which always produces its small purple feathered blooms on
Christmas Day. A few flowers brought into the house then, are worth any
number of Christmas bangles.

The Late Starter

by Neil Williams

As a young man, gardening was never a priority and for many years cutting grass was about my limit. When Sonia and I married in 1964, we lived in Colchester, Essex and bought a house with a totally overgrown garden, previously owned by a retired alcoholic army colonel. While Sonia had been a keen gardener from her youth, this was my introduction to the joys of gardening.

One of my first jobs was to prune the overgrown Hydrangeas and I cut them within an inch of their lives to Sonia's horror. We returned from England in 1969 and bought Carewswood which we ran as a fruit and vegetable farm for several years but always had the desire to open a Garden Centre at some stage. This did not happen until 1982 and was the turning point of our lives. We spent the first two years studying the available plants, their habits and growing conditions.

Overnight I became a total plantaholic and have remained one ever since. Every Spring I drove to the U.K. to locate and buy plants which were not available in Ireland and during that time we introduced several plants which were unknown here; in fact we were one of the first Garden Centres to have tree ferns for sale. The business was very successful and took over our lives, but we never had time to do much gardening for ourselves although we did a limited amount of landscaping for customers.

In 1996 we decided to retire and sold Carewswood as a going concern. The house we bought at that time had two acres of ground, totally uncultivated, part of which was grazing a herd of cattle; exactly what we wanted – a blank canvas and a big challenge. This was the period in my life when I became a real gardener and since then I have learned more about the habits and requirements of plants than I ever knew before. Obviously my knowledge of plants over the years was a great asset. How to put them together was the problem. We started off with many straight lines and as the garden developed, these became curves and sweeps. What a fascinating hobby this gardening is. It keeps one's body fit and one's mind active.

Every year we make changes and every year we buy more plants and find new homes for them. I say we because this is not my garden but *our* garden, and without Sonia's input it would not be as good as it is. I have not cut grass for 9 years! This job is jealously guarded by Sonia.

Sonia also has a great eye for colour and design and we always plan new areas together. To garden alone would never be as interesting but when both partners are keen it is a very fulfilling hobby. The garden is open to the public from May To September by appointment and we have had many lovely visitors over the years from Ireland, the UK, as well as Holland, France and Germany.

I Love Salvias

by Bob Brown

I love salvias. The plants are so neat, flower from May (or sometimes even April) till the end of July here in Worcestershire and then flower (a little) again on side branches until frosts take hold. When the flowers have finished, the bracts (and sometimes leaves) are often colourful and I can get another two months of effect out of them. The form of the plants and spires of flower mean that even the dead heads look ok for a month or two in the winter. They are trouble-free and persist even through cold wet winters. Show me a tender or borderline hardy salvia with as much payback, please.

The best is *Salvia nemorosa* 'Carradonna'. It has deep purple spires of flower on black stems. Sadly it was marketed after the RHS trials so it has no award. Almost as good are *Salvia nemorosa* 'Amethyst' AGM and 'Sensation Rose' (also a new arrival). I object to the squatness of *Salvia nemorosa* 'Marcus' but if you like dwarfs it's for you. *Salvia nemorosa* 'Plumosa' AGM has no petals (or sepals) but only double bracts, which, of course, do not get fertilized, and drop off but persist for ages. The trouble is, the plant lacks form – it can degenerate into shapeless blobs. Varieties of *Salvia x superba* AGM and *Salvia x sylvestris* look and behave in similar ways. My personal favourite is *Salvia x sylvestris* 'Lye End'. One of the parents of *Salvia x sylvestris* is *Salvia pratensis* – the meadow clary, and 'Lye End' has the same relatively big blue flowers with great impact over a shorter period than *Salvia nemorosa* varieties. My stock was given to me by Primrose Upward who inherited Lye End Nurseries from that great plants woman Miss Pole, so its provenance is impeccable!

Salvia nemorosa 'Carradonna'

An enormous swarm of salvias respond to heat in order to grow and flower.
I think they all originate from either North or South America. This is fine
in Alabama, even in Maine or Toronto, but here in the cool NW of Europe
summer heat is often late in coming, unreliable in intensity and duration.
So, *Salvia guaranitica* 'Black and Blue' (now dead) often did not appear above
ground till July and got frosted off long before even the flower buds began
to form. I tried keeping it in pots inside until May, then planting it out and
achieved flowers in October - dark indigo blue from black calyces, but at three
metres they were silhouettes, which would appear black even if they were
yellow. I was advised to try a lower-flowering and hardier form 'Blue Enigma'
AGM. It was planted three times but it always died in the ground overwinter.
Maybe winters are too warm here in Worcestershire? I do listen. Two great
friends are very experienced gardeners and always have a magnificent show
of *Salvia splendens* 'Van-Houttei' AGM for their garden open day in July. It
behaves for them like a bedding salvia (*Salvia splendens*) on steroids - all red and
black (and green). It is a tender shrub normally grown as a half-hardy annual.
Maybe I should have started it into growth in January under heat. This at least
might have meant it was tough enough to be mollusc-proof by the time they
appear from hibernation in April and May. It died (of snails). *Salvia mexicana*
'Limelight' described as 'Lovely pendulous pale greeny-yellow heads with
purple flowers' by its (kind) donor, tried to flower in late November inside the
protection of an unheated tunnel before it too, died.
At least I enjoyed the scented foliage of *Salvia rutilans* (prostrate form). It is best not
to openly discuss anything with the word 'prostrate' in public. Flowers promised for
autumn never appeared. *Salvia semiatrata* had the look of a hardy plant that might
survive outside in the Midlands (of England). Mmm…

One salvia I endeavour never to be without is *Salvia uliginosa*. Pure clear
pale blue is an unusual late summer (and autumn) colour and this plant gives it
in profusion. I once planted it in a public garden where it overwhelmed several
shrubs (to death) but drew gasps of admiration from visitors. You see, it runs.
It is herbaceous and grows up to about two metres tall then falls. It likes wet

summers and dry winters. Wet summers and dry winters? Yes, wet summers and dry winters. How it survived long enough to overwhelm anything I'll never understand. The British Isles do not do wet summers and dry winters. They can do wet winters and dry summers but that's no substitute. It is also reckoned to be tenderish (it is from Argentina and Uruguay) but if kept dry in pots I have found it can be successfully frozen.

Salvia aurea 'Kirstenbosch'

I have it from time to time and will continue to replant it when it disappears. Eight out of ten! I also persist in growing another problematical salvia, *Salvia aurea* 'Kirstenbosch'. This has clove-scented leaves (a nice smell if it didn't remind me of childhood toothache). The leaves are silvery grey and are densely held on a well-formed shrub that I grow in a big pot and protect from frost. In April, May and June it has large brown flowers, which would look perfect in the fashionable dead-looking garden, looking dead (as they do) from the moment they open. Nay, even in bud. If it gets at all gawky or too big for its pot, I have discovered it responds well to stooling. I take visitors to see it. I was encouraged by its South African provenance and obtained seed of *Salvia dentata*. This is untidy and boring with conventional pale blue flowers - it got planted

out to kill it. You'd never suspect I was such a pussycat, would you?
It took two winters.

Apart from temperature dependent flowers, another frequent problem
with American salvias is their shape. Many of them are twiggy (dead twiggy)
and gawky. I do not think it is the way that I grow them but more damningly,
it's in their nature to regrow the following season some distance behind where
they finished flowering the season before. They end up looking like bird's nests
or jasmine (but not as bad as jasmine). Inertia and winter hardiness mean I
still have *Salvia* 'Maraschino' and *Salvia* 'Raspberry Royale' which have two
flushes of red flowers in April and May and again in the autumn. These have
this problem. This group of twiggy salvias have another problem (shared with

Salvia 'Maraschino'

Geranium x oxonianum cultivars),
which is that the flowers are never
concentrated enough for serious
garden impact. A flower here,
and there's one here, and look!
There's another one here. *Salvia*
'Maraschino' is better than *Salvia
greggii* (one of its parents). I believe
Salvia greggii comes from Texas
and I can just visualise a landscape
of hot, flat, dry scrubland dusted
with gusty winds and *Salvia greggii*.
Salvia greggii 'Desert Blaze' has
a nice combination of white-
edged grey-green leaves and large
maroon-scarlet flowers between
April and October. It grows to
about 65cm. The originator was
John Augustine from Phoenix, Arizona. It is hardy in the English Midlands
only trembling at -16C in open ground in November 2005. As chairman of

the Variegated Plant Group of the Hardy Plant Society I continue to grow it despite diffused flowering and twiggyness. *Salvia greggii* has cultivars for every taste even a combination of repellent pink and yellow in the form 'Peach'. Then there's *Salvia arizonica* - which says it all!

Of course *Salvia nemorosa* (native to lands stretching from Europe to Central Asia) is not the only hardy Eurasian species. Sage itself is tough enough to survive 29 out of 30 winters here in Worcestershire (I guess). I lost it and all of its cultivars and the related species *Salvia lavandulifolia* in the winter of 1982/3 (when I lived in Surrey) because of the very low and persistent temperatures. 'Icterina' seems to be the most tender and 'Berggarten' the toughest. These have the advantage of foliage that is not only good with onion and chicken, but also, that looks good for much of the year. Sadly *Salvia candelabrum* (which must be a close relative) hates to grow on my clay but survives well in more open soils. I really like its airy purple flower heads, which have something in common with lavender - but less densely so!

However, apart from *Salvia nemorosa* and its hybrids and sage and its relatives, most of the Eurasian species are not very garden worthy. *Salvia glutinosa* (3/10) has greyed pale yellow flowers from an ugly adhesive plant dotted with dead black insect corpses. *Salvia austriaca* is similar with pinky-brown additions to the yellow in the flower. Yuck! *Salvia multicaulis* (5/10) hit the gardening public in the early 1990s but seems to have more or less disappeared now. Its attraction were the clusters of persistent large dark purple, cup-shaped calyces, but they require high concentrations of UV light to colour well (like you get in Syria and Lebanon). Limerick, Cumbria and Worcestershire get poorer results. I think mine died from winter wet. Although Syria and Lebanon and much of the Mediterranean is wet in winter, there's wet and wet, and days of dark wet with high relative humidity in between rain. This was probably too much for the plants. Then there's the *Salvia turkestanica/moorcroftiana/tomentosa/forsskaolii/przewalskii* swarm, which I mentally group together as, 'basal rosettes, branched spires at flowering, hairy, not colourful, wet problems (any season)'. These score an average 4/10.

All this diatribe!

Some salvias may be tender but they are still worth growing. *Salvia leucantha* AGM with its white flowers from persistent downy purple calyces and nice corrugated leaves, white downy beneath, is lovely. So is *Salvia farinacea* 'Victoria' AGM and *Salvia patens* AGM (any shade of blue you desire for late summer) is a delight and so easy to overwinter as a tuber.

To conclude, I must write that I am very happy to protect plants overwinter (or whenever they need it) but they must repay the expense and trouble by having fairly overwhelming benefits. So, for *Cantua buxifolia* 'Dancing Oaks' it is six or eight weeks of superlative rich dripping arterial red flowers in thick bunches. For *Bouvardia ternifolia* it is seven to eight months of continuous vermilion flowers in many-flowered clusters at the ends of branches looking straight up at me. For *Aeonium* 'Zwartkop' it is the shining rosettes of black evergreen foliage. For *Clivia miniata* it is the utter ease of growing it and its supreme shade tolerance and shapeliness. For *Lachenalia viridiflora* it's the incredible turquoise flower in November and December. Wow! Sadly salvias on the whole do not qualify and I am left cold by the boundless enthusiasm of gardeners and (even famous) plantsmen who I would expect to be more discriminating. Maybe it is the smell of the foliage that hypnotises them?

Reminiscence

by Carl Dacus

At the end of January I was asked by Jim Dennison to submit an article for the LGPG on their tenth anniversary, I immediately recalled a number of very pleasant evenings spent in front of a slide projector in Limerick.

My initial contact was through Stephen Redden who was then the manager in Van Veen's and had bought many plants from my nursery for their garden centre. My interest was in propagation and in particular from seed, more so if the seed came from obscure regions/sources and if from previously unheard of plants, so much the better.

As can be imagined it is quite difficult to make a living from the resulting material but through a few adventurous nurseries including Van Veen's and later Stephen's Hillberry nursery in Crecora it became possible to provide a range of plants rarely or not previously available to the adventurous gardener.

Shortly after preliminary contacts with Van Veen's, Stephen asked me if I would agree to give a talk to the LGPG and bring along a range of plants including alpines, herbaceous perennials, roses, etc for sale. Many of the plants had been grown from seeds from John Watson (South America) Ron Ratco (NW USA), Josef Halda (former USSR), Jim and Jenny Archibald (from world wide and cultivated) to mention but some of my seed sources and, of course, plant material donated by gardening friends or local plant sales. My memory is a little hazy but I think that I gave three most enjoyable talks mainly on my own garden, in which roses, alpines, aquatics and herbaceous perennials featured.

The following are some of the plants which I would have brought to Limerick over the years:

Vallea stipularis: This came to me from a well known gardener in Dublin. It produces small pink flowers early in the year on a tall rather lank shrub, for me a must!

Rhododendron 'St. Breward': A very beautiful small/medium sized evergreen shrub with soft lavender flowers of a good size, as *R. augustinii* is one of the parents it has a little tolerance to a higher pH than most Rhododendrons, another must have.

Hypericum 'Rowallane': this plant came from my grandmother's garden
and as far as I know, I was the only one to propagate it in Ireland. This is a
superb plant forming in mild climates, an evergreen shrub to two metres,
flowering throughout most of the year with 5-7.5 centimetre flowers of
rich yellow. Hillier's state: "This magnificent semi-evergreen plant is the
finest of the genus but needs a sheltered site."

Rosa 'Belvedere': Strong growing rambler once flowering with very
large clusters of double soft pink non-scented flowers prone to mildew,
discovered by Graham Stuart Thomas in Ireland. I supplied the original
stock plants growing in Belvedere House, Mullingar. It is most noteworthy
when in full flower.

Rosa x odorata 'Pseudindica' ('Fortune's Double Yellow'): a very old tea rose
collected by Robert Fortune in a mandarin's garden in Ningpo, China.
Again, this rose was discovered by Graham Stuart Thomas in an Irish
garden and reintroduced to cultivation in the UK and via Fionnuala Reid
to me. This rose grows in a lean-to glasshouse producing strong growths
covered in flowers through the vents; the flowers have a very delicate tea
scent. Stephen has grown it outside in Limerick over a number of years.

Rosa x odorata 'Bengal Crimson': Of all the roses in this article, this one
flowers continuously, crimson in summer and pink in winter. The flowers
are single with no scent making a disease free a bush one and a half metre
high or on a wall up to five metre.

Rosa laevigata 'Cooperi' 'Cooper's Burmese Rose', if space permits, makes
a wonderful evergreen climber with very large single scented white
flowers turning pink when pollinated shown off well by the dark green
leaves, flowering in early summer.

Bomarea caldasii and *B. patacocensis* are first class and spectacular climbers.
They produce annual growths over 2 metre high with clusters of orange
flowers in frost free climates over the year. In more normal conditions
they flower in the autumn. My stock originated from Jim Archibald who
collected the seeds in Ecuador. Offspring of these plants are available from

Kilmurray Nurseries (Orla and Paul Woods).

Kniphofia northiae from seed collected by Charles Nelson and Jim Archibald.
It has proven to be a spectacular plant both in foliage and flower.

Daphne's have always been popular to gardeners, and for me *Daphne collina* is hard to beat; it forms a dwarf evergreen shrub which flowers in spring and again in the autumn with rose-purple, highly scented flowers. All daphnes should be considered as short lived plants.

I will now cover a few plants which may be used in the alpine garden:

Aethionema grandiflorum: An easy to grow plant covered with scented pink flowers in early summer on eight inch stems. It self seeds in a mild way around the mother plant, well worth growing.

Alyssum spinosum 'Roseum': Another plant with pink flowers above a silver leaved sub-shrub in early summer, foliage looks well all year.

Anthyllis vulneraria var. coccinea is a short lived prostrate member of the pea family with brilliant scarlet flowers over summer, it gently self seeds and is best on a sunny well drained site.

Dianthus 'Pikes Pink' with highly scented pink flowers on four to six inch stems forming a neat and compact plant.

Diplarrhena moraea is a very beautiful member of the Iridaceae. This plant comes from Tasmania, is summer flowering and grows well in a slightly acidic soil with good drainage. The flowers are white and scented. My stock originated from an RHSI plant sale many years ago and, if my memory serves me correctly, was donated by Helen Dillon and David Shackleton.

Dudleya cymosa subsp: I grew a number of different Dudleya's, all grown from seed supplied by Ron Ratco, collected from high altitudes in California. These plants performed well in a hot well drained raised bed. The flowers are yellow/orange above silver rosettes. They are well worth growing.

Hieracium lanatum: A hawkweed is an easily grown plant with a most wonderful silver foliage. The strongly coloured yellow flowers may be removed before they open, leaving just a few to produce seed for new plants.

Zauschneria californica in the form 'Western Hills'.

The Zauschneria's are excellent late summer to late autumn, producing masses of scarlet flowers which, in this form, are shown off to advantage above the silver foliage. As this plant is a strong grower it may swamp other more refined plants.

It is most important that societies like the LGPG thrive and cultivate an interest in plants; the danger today is that the multiples will only supply a limited range of plants, in many cases incompletely or wrongly named.

These major societies across the country are providing an excellent service to real plants-people. Keep up the good work and bring in many specialist nurserymen to share their experience and plants with us. Continue the good work in Limerick and I thank you for the opportunity to bring some new and unusual plants to your city, and look forward to the next ten years!

My Gertrude Jekyll Garden

by Rosamund Wallinger

In July 1983, my husband John came back from work and announced that we were going to sell our small but comfortable London house and move to the country. Confident that this was a passing whim I agreed; and that was the start of our great garden adventure.

Among the details of houses on the market that arrived daily was a cheap black and white page describing a Grade II historic 'part Jacobean' house in north-east Hampshire. The house too was surprisingly cheap and on investigation we discovered why. It had been on the market for well over two years; it had stood virtually empty for five, and in those years rot, woodworm and damp had invaded it. We found forty-six burst pipes; it needed re-wiring and repairs to the roof. It transpired that the seller had been trying, but had failed, to get planning permission to build 14 cottages in the five acre garden.

After a little haggling on both sides we bought the Manor House in December 1983. Wondering why, what looked like to us a decaying Mock Tudor house, described as part Jacobean was listed Grade II, John and I went to the RIBA (Royal Institute of British Architects) in London to investigate. There we learnt that our house was listed, not because of its old foundations, but because in 1902 an important Arts and Crafts figure, Charles Holme, founder of The Studio magazine, had commissioned the architect Ernest Newton to carry out what was described as 'alterations and additions to the Old Manor House. At the bottom of a full description of both Holme and Newton the concluding line simply stated 'Garden possibly Gertrude Jekyll.'

In April 1984 we moved in to our large, damp, cold Manor House, having sent our son off to nice warm boarding school for most of the summer. The garden of the Manor House was in even worse state than the house. In the formal garden, drystone walls were largely collapsed and encased with weeds. There was no sign of original flower beds, pergola, tennis arbour, lawn or bowling lawn but, because of neglect, nothing had been built where those should stand. The Wild garden was truly wild. We could hardly walk through the weeds, incorrect trees and brambles, and the once spring-fed pond had

long since dried up and disappeared. Very soon, several garden historians and
horticultural bodies rallied around encouraging us to buy copies of Miss
Jekyll's 19 original plans from the University of Berkeley where they are now
held and advising us just how to go about restoring her 1908 masterpiece.

★Manor House

Having never gardened before, the plans, when they did arrive, were like
documents in a foreign language. But with the help of horticulturists including
Penelope Hobhouse, Richard Bisgrove and Michael Tooley, who were fast
becoming friends, we deciphered and then ordered the correct shrubs, flowers
and trees. We had little money left after virtually re-building the house. Our first
job was to totally clear the garden and then burn or dig in the rubbish we had
accumulated. Later that year I ordered seeds of as many of Jekyll's plants that
I could. Shrubs and trees were bought as small and inexpensively as possible
and where I had to buy a plant or rootstock I bought fewer than on the plans

and divided them over the following years.

It was the re-building of the drystone walls and repairing stone terraces that was the biggest expense. After that the hiring and then buying of necessary garden machinery, chain saw, tractor, cylinder mowers and all the digging and raking pieces used up the rest of our funds. I learnt almost all the anguish-making lessons of an amateur gardener in the first few years at Upton Grey. I poisoned valuable plants with what I thought was fly killer – but was Roundup. I drowned and then scorched seedlings as I tried to grow them with no shelter. In 1987 we put up a small do-it-yourself-with lots-of-bad-language-greenhouse and that made growing from seed easier.

I soon learnt that tall herbaceous plants like helianthus and helenium don't stand up on their own throughout summer storms and had tearfully learnt to prop them up with stakes made from trees in the Nuttery. By 1989 I was beginning to think we had a really beautiful Gertrude Jekyll garden. But really only the formal, herbaceous part of the garden was at all pretty and even there, surrounding yew hedges were still short stumps. The shape was fine in the centre but around the edges the garden was still dishevelled. The Wild Garden, I knew, would take several years to look like a Jekyll garden. Trees and large shrubs had to grow to form woodland glades and meandering paths, but the Wild Garden never looked a mess; it just started gently like a late developing child and it is till maturing into a splendid beauty.

Today, 24 years after its resurrection, Miss Jekyll's garden really is a tribute to her enduring art. Gardeners come from around the world to see how that art is still admired, one hundred years after she planned it. It is thanks to the nurseries of Britain that we have been able to find almost all of her original plants and it is because she chose simple, reliable plants for her clients, plants that, when planted in large drifts moved colour and structure across the borders in crescendos of cool blues and white to vibrant reds – rather like crescendos in music.

Miss Jekyll was a pioneer in using many facets of art in her gardens. She combined the formal styles of the architectural gardeners with the free, natural styles of gardeners like William Robinson. Like many conflicts in art, gardeners had divided into two camps, writing venomously of each other's art as being either vulgar and wriggling ,or laid out like colourful tarts on a pastry-cook's tray. Miss Jekyll, seeing sermons in stones and good in almost anything in nature, wrote 'both are right and both are wrong but they ignore the beauty in each other's art.' We should remember that today.

Modern gardens are very fine and often beautifully complimentary to modern architecture, but there is a place for just a very few restorations of past garden art so that we can judge that art and learn to move on. Miss Jekyll was well aware that art is not static, that it must evolve, and she wrote as much.

I have learnt a great deal through gardening and have made many wise friends. Looking out over this garden Miss Jekyll's words resound in my memory. She was an artist and a gardener. 'Planting the ground', she wrote, 'is painting the landscape with living things.'

Image of Manor House taken, with permission, from:
'Gertrude Jekyll's Lost Garden'
by Rosamund Wallinger
Published in 2000 by Garden Art Press

Restios

by Phemie Rose

Elegia capensis-this was the plant which began my fascination with the restio family. The Restionaceae is a family of rush-like plants largely from the southern hemisphere. The Restionaceae is a typical 'southern' or 'austral' plant family. It is found on all the southern continents, with ca.330 species in Africa, ca.150 species in Australia, 4 species in New Zealand, a single species in South America and a single species widespread in South East Asia. Restios can be found in virtually all habitats of the South African fynbos, from sandy plains to mountain summits and from very dry places to seasonally wet or permanent marshes. However they cannot be found in aquatic habitats, and are also absent from the forest understorey.

There are very large and very small species. *Cannomois gigantea* can reach heights of twelve foot or more. *Calopsis paniculata,* as pictured, is definitely not for the small garden. On the right hand side of the picture you can just see the seed heads of *Thamnochortus insignis* with its slender stems which wave gently in the wind. It is used for thatching in its native South Africa. Others such as *Ischyrolepis sieberi* make an attractive mound about three foot high. Square stems distinguish *Restio quadratus* from other species forming great clumps up to five foot high with branched culms which droop at the tips.

Calopsis paniculata

Of the South African restios, I am growing 30 different species. I am also growing three Australian species and one New Zealand species. Most of them I have grown from seed and I am continually on the look out for seed from Australia, New Zealand, South America and Asia as seeds from these countries are very hard to come by.

Restios are wind pollinated, so I am experimenting at the moment having planted a male *Elegia capensis* upwind of a female *Elegia capensis*. I have collected seed but as to whether it is viable or not only time will tell. Males and females of the same species can look very alike or very different. Identifying them is a nightmare, as are the names.

The Australian species that I am growing (*Balaskion tetraphyllum*, which was *Restio tetraphyllus*, *Balaskion australe*, which was *Restio australis* and *Tremulina tremula* which was *Restio tremulus*) are much smaller and more delicate than their South African cousins.

Restio tetraphyllus

I have succeeded in germinating only one seed of the packet of *Leptocarpus similis* so it is very special. I have not even seen a photograph of it, so I am observing its growth very carefully.

Restios are not easy to germinate. Best germination is achieved by treating the seeds with 'smoke primers' (which I buy from Kirstenbosch Botanic Gardens, South Africa) prior to planting and when they experience a marked difference (around 8°C) between day and night temperatures after they are sown. After germination I place them outside where they will get sun and lots of air movement, this improves their growth rate significantly. They appreciate acid soils which are of low fertility, and they do not appreciate phosphorus. During their first year the seedlings look very different from the adult plants and have numerous finely-branched sterile culms. This bushy sterile growth probably maximises photosynthesis. In the second winter a new set of culms is made and the first year's growth dies back. Only in the third year do the plants reach their typical adult shape and form.

Restio festuciformis is a lovely low growing plant with delicate bright green culms and lovely golden seed heads. They are of great value in the garden both from their architectural form and year round presence. They look just as good in winter as they do in summer. Some of them are very large, making great cut foliage, with individual stems that can last for months in water.

Restio festuciformis

If you have alkaline soil they can also be grown in pots. They need sun, air movement and plenty of water. Also, because they are fast growers, they need to be potted on frequently. They resent root disturbance and can sulk for three or four years after being moved, or worse still, split.

The Belfast Botanic Gardens

by Reg Maxwell

Belfast at the beginning of the nineteenth century was a small port at the mouth of Belfast Lough, with the rural farming community right to the edge of town. Within fifty years it would become a thriving industrial town, the population rising from 30,000 in 1831 to almost 200,000 in 1871.

The burgeoning middle class, as elsewhere in Europe, began to form seats of learning; Belfast Royal Academy was established in 1785 and Belfast Academical Institute in 1810. It was suggested that a botany department be added to the latter, and in 1814 we find a certain John Templeton advocating the creation of a botanical garden beside the school. However the ground was found to be unsuitable.

John Templeton was a botanist/gardener who lived at Cranmore on the Malone Road. There he built up a fine collection of trees and plants. He was born in Belfast in 1766 and spent a lifetime botanising in the greater Belfast area. He is noted for his finding of *Orobanche alba var. rubra*, a saprophyte that grows on thyme. I have only seen this once, growing on the Cavehill in 1972, on the thyme banks along the line of the old deer park wall of Belfast Castle. He identified and named *Rosa x hibernica* growing in a hedge line near Hollywood Co. Down in 1795. In the 1960s due to a road widening scheme, this plant was lifted and put in the little botanic collection at Derryvolgie, a Queens University garden. It was moved again in the late 1980s to the rose gardens in the Botanic Gardens as the Derryvolgie site was going for redevelopment. It is fitting that Templeton's rose is in the garden that he so wished to see. Templeton was a great friend of Lord Clanbrassil of Tollymore, which in the late 18th and 19th century was a garden of distinction. It was through this friendship that Templeton came to the notice of Sir Joseph Banks who wanted him to go to Australia botanising. He would not however leave his native Ireland. The Genus Templetonia, native to Australia, is named in his honour. Templeton did not live to see a Belfast Botanical Garden established, as he died in 1825.

The Belfast Natural History and Philosophical Society, founded in 1821, undertook to develop a botanical garden and issued a prospectus in

February of 1827. In that year they obtained two acres of land at the Malone turnpike, now Shaftsbury Square, and employed a gardener. The society's corresponding secretary, James MacAdam, was already making contact with other gardens and plant collectors in different parts of the world. One such person who was well placed to help with the supply of exotic seeds and plants was Charles Telfair, a Belfast man. He was a surgeon botanist in Port Louis, Mauritius. He established a botanic garden there, and sent back plants and seeds to Belfast on the understanding that a portion must also be sent to Dr. William Hooker at Glasgow Botanic Garden.

A founder member of the Belfast Botanical Gardens was Edmond Getty (1799 -1857). He was in the service of the Belfast Ballast Board where he became Master in 1837 and when the Board became the Harbour Commissioners in 1847 he held the post of Chief Executive. His connection with Queen's Island and the Botanics has been mixed up in Belfast folk lore. I remember in the early 1970s being informed by the older generation of visitors to the Palm House that the Palm House had come from Queens Island. This of course was not true. The connection was that Getty had a Winter Garden on the Island in which there was a collection of plants and a menagerie.

Edmund Getty, along with other members of the Belfast Natural History and Philosophical Society formed the Belfast Botanical Society which in 1828 purchased the lands known as White Course, now the present Botanic Gardens. The land at the time was a farm but interestingly it had been a nursery in the 1780s and 90s. It had a good stock of trees and springs, at that time essential for a water supply. The Society advertised in Loudon's Garden Magazine in January 1828 for a curator.

The first curator was Thomas Drummond from Scotland. He had been the assistant naturalist to Sir John Franklin's Arctic expedition of 1825-27. His father was gardener at Fotheringham Estate, Forfar. His brother James was Curator of Cork Botanic Gardens. Drummond laid out the gardens and prepared for planting by August 1828 as he reported to Dr. Hooker in that month. The path systems of today are much as he laid out. He was able to grow some of the

plants from seed he had collected on the Arctic expedition, and send some
of this material to Hooker. Sadly, Drummond did not get on well with the
Society and Mrs Templeton wrote to Dr. Hooker on his behalf to help him to
go on another plant hunting expedition to North America. He left Belfast in
January 1831 and was in Boston by April of that year. Drummond botanised
through the eastern states of America, sending 700 species back from Texas.
He will be remembered for one particular plant, sent in one of the last
shipments: 'Texas Pride' or *Phlox drummondii*, a well known garden plant.
Sadly, he died in Cuba and was never able to provide for his family as he had
hoped. There followed, as curators, three other Scots in quick succession:
Bishop from Perthshire, Campbell whose father was head gardener at Pollock
House in Glasgow, and Daniel Ferguson.

Sir Charles Lanyon's Palm House

Ferguson was to see the greatest developments in the gardens during
his tenure from 1836 to 1864. He had worked at Glasgow Botanical Garden
under Dr. Hooker and the curator, Mr Murray. The Belfast Gardens were now
receiving plants from all parts of the empire and in one large shipment from

Australasia, specimens of *Telopea speciosissima*. *Lagunaria patersonii* and *Doryanthes excelsa* were received. Doryanthes makes a fine conservatory plant and after the renovation of the Belfast Palm House in 1980 I obtained a specimen from Kew Gardens. This plant was grown in a large pot and was used at a number of major flower shows in Scotland and England until it became to large. It is called the Spear Lily, alluding to its large strap-shaped leaves. When it was 25 years old it produced a seven metre flower spike that had hundreds of bright red flowers full of nectar. With a little bit of careful hand pollinating, twenty one seed heads were formed and a good crop of new plants have been established. The records do not show if the first plants of 1838 ever flowered. It was very satisfying to have re-introduced a plant that had been in the gardens a hundred and thirty years before.

The 1830s saw a huge influx of tropical plants and the only display houses were the Orchid and Fern House. The Society moved to build a conservatory and engaged the architect Sir Charles Lanyon who designed the present Palm House. Work started in 1839 and the two wings were built by the Dublin ironmaster William Turner and completed in 1840. The glass was supplied by Walker of Dublin. The first glass was corded on the inside. The objective was to defuse the suns rays to stop scorching of the plants. The idea was good but it failed to work as the grooves filled with dirt and algae which cut out the light. It was replaced with clear glass. We still have a stock of the original corded glass. The structure of the Palm House is cast and wrought iron. The use of iron gave a much lighter and graceful house as opposed to the wooden house that went before. The dome was not built until 1852 and it was by Young of Edinburgh. The wings cost £1400 and the dome £1000. Daniel Ferguson obtained plants from Glasgow, Edinburgh and Kew to help stock the new Palm House. In 1853 he brought to flower the giant water lily *Victoria amazonica* for the first time in Ireland, in a specially constructed house at the rear of the Palm House. Ferguson left one of the best records of the gardens in his guide, published in 1851. It recorded the species in the collections as well as details of the features of the gardens. Ferguson was succeeded by his son William Hooker Ferguson who stayed for only four years.

The next curator was Joseph Forsyth Johnson who came from the Manchester Botanic Gardens. He changed the way the garden was to develop. On his arrival he was dismissive of the current management, stating that 'the gardens were deficient in all classes of plants and general decoration'. As recorded in his annual curators report to the Society, he produced that year 200,000 bedding type plants. These were used in the part of the garden in front of the Palm House which to this day is still the flower garden. While at Belfast he wrote 'The Natural Principles of Landscape Gardening' (1874). This he later put into practice when, after leaving Belfast, he went to England, then America, where he worked in Atlanta, Georgia and North Carolina, landscaping public parks.

The last curator was Charles McKimm (1877-1907) born in Donaghadee, Co. Down. He did his training at Lord Farnhams estate, Co. Cavan, and came to the gardens in 1877. In 1887 he embarked on his most famous project, the Tropical Ravine. This house was built over the old Orchid and Fern Houses and covered a small glen. The design was imaginative in that he created features that would entertain the visitor as well as display exotic plants. Grottoes, waterfalls, caves, mirrors and water-worn stone steps all adding to the experience of seeing tropical plants from all parts of the world growing lushly together.

In 1895 the Society sold the Gardens to Belfast Corporation for £10,500 when it became a public garden, open and free to all. McKimm stayed on as curator and the first Superintendent of Parks. He was still to make his mark on the Gardens. By 1900 he had extended the Tropical Ravine to what it is today: two sections, stove and temperate, giving Belfast a unique glasshouse. There are today a number of the original McKimm plants, all growing happily in the Tropical Ravine: *Cycad spp*, *Encephalartos spp*, *Stenocarpus sinuatus* and *Musa spp*.

Another great feature introduced to the gardens by McKimm, and in constant use since 1900, is the herbaceous border. There are four borders each 150 meters long; three are herbaceous and one grasses and bamboo. The top

borders have seven arches created in cement to look like wood, an interesting
design and especially charming when the climbers are covered in flower.
There are two other major features which give structure to the gardens; one is
the limestone rockery area constructed in 1918-1920; only the path systems,
stream and some of the conifers are left. The second feature, the rose gardens,
were created in 1930. There is a central pergola with bluestone pillars and
path, and beds of roses on either side, mainly cultivars raised by Dickson and
McReedy; 8,000 plants give a wonderful display each summer.

The gardens have some fine old trees: *Carpinus betulus* 'Asplenifolia,'
C. betulus 'Quercicifolia', *Quercus canariensis, Q ilex* 'Fordii', all from the
1860s planting. From more recent times, there is a fine specimen of
Metasequoia glyptostroboides which may be the third largest in Ireland, and the
last introduction of note is the Willime pine.

The history of Belfast Botanic Gardens is about plants and people
creating a beautiful place. Our present footfall is over 70,000 visitors each year,
people enjoying a walk through or attending events. It is a tribute to the
work of gardeners over the years that in spite of this heavy use, the gardens
have maintained the collections, specimen plants and features for future
generations to enjoy.

My Garden

by Carmel Duignan

When, on a cold brisk day in October 1987, I clambered over a
crumbling wall to get a first glimpse of my future garden, I was less
than impressed by the litter-stewn, upward-sloping, bleak field I beheld. I was
then in a rhododendron-loving stage and, not only was my new garden a mess,
it was also very alkaline (like most of Dublin). However, I discovered very soon
that I had found something better than acid soil: a warm sheltered site close to
the sea but far enough away from it to escape the salt and the wind. By trial
and accident, I found that I could grow tender plants out of doors and I was
now onto something that beat rhododendrons hands down.

The garden is about a quarter of an acre and the soil is heavy, alkaline
clay with a PH of 7.4. It gets quite wet in winter and dries out like concrete in
summer. Rainfall is relatively low with an annual precipitation of about
26 inches. Primulas, meconopsis and other moisture-loving plants will not do
here as it is much too dry. Temperatures in winter rarely go lower than -2° C.
The garden is south-facing and slopes upwards. It is terraced with a lawn in
the centre and double borders on each side.

My first experiment in tender plants was with *Acacia baileyana* 'Purpurea'. I got the seed from Chilterns in England, sowed them carefully and watched over the only two seedlings that survived. One was finally planted out and, over the years, made a fine spreading tree. It was my favourite plant, beautiful in all seasons and the same age as the garden. However, on 7th January of this year we had a big wind and the next morning I found my beautiful tree, in full flower, lying on the lawn. It had sheared off at the base and is now drying out to be fuel for my living room fire next winter. Such is the joy and sorrow of gardening.

I saw my first pseudopanax many years ago in a small garden centre perched on the edge of the Atlantic Ocean in County Galway. It was love at first sight, not that the object of my affection was a thing of beauty. *Pseudopanax crassifolius*, when young, has long, leathery leaves that droop downward from the stem and look like the spokes of a half-closed umbrella. This is the juvenile foliage and it is a trait found in other plants from New Zealand. When the plant matures, at about 17 years old, the leaves become short and more leaf-like, more branches develop and the overall effect is of a slender, lollipop-shaped small tree. I grow many different species and varieties of pseudopanax and most of them start off life with regular leaves. *Pseudopanax lessonii* 'Trident' is a particular favourite. It makes an elegant, narrow, multi-stemmed small tree of 5-6 metres with three-lobed, trident-like, glossy leaves and a beautifully patterned bark. 'Gold Splash' is a smaller shrub to 3 metres high and wide. The evergreen leaves are liberally splashed with gold along the veins and midribs. These plants are very much hardier than is generally believed and would grow very well in city gardens where microclimates are created by nearby buildings and lighting. They are rewarding plants, are completely trouble-free, will grow in any soil and create an easy, exotic effect.

Bleddyn & Sue Wynn Jones of Crûg Farm Plants (www.crug-farm. co.uk) have introduced many remarkable plants and none more so than *Schefflera taiwaniana*. From Taiwan, this beautiful plant will grow to 3-4 metres high and has survived unscathed in North Wales for over ten winters.

Pale-green, shuttlecock-like, folded leaves emerge on tall stalks in spring and gradually widen and darken to become glossy-green, outstretched leaflets held on elegant long stems. Another amazing plant from the same stable is *Schefflera macrophylla* from Vietnam. The long, paddle-shaped leaves grow to a metre long and the new growth is pale green and covered with orange indumentum. It has survived temperatures of -10° at Crûg Farm. These two lovely plants need no pampering, they toughen it out in my crowded borders with more mundane neighbours and they do so effortlessly.

Tetrapanax 'Rex', courtesy of Deborah Begley

Tetrapanax papyrifera or the rice paper plant is much hardier than its tropical appearance suggests. The variety 'Rex' has huge palmate leaves that grow to over a metre long. Indeed this plant should come with a health warning. It will produce suckers that could form a thicket within a short time if left unattended. Usually, I have no problem with the suckers. I pot them up and have no difficulty in finding homes for them.

Lately, I have become very interested in the more tender species Fuchsia. I grow *F. paniculata* and *F. bolivana* outdoors and they take on a herbaceous habit, dying down in winter and recovering each spring. I particularly like 'Gesneriana', thought to be an inter-species hybrid between *F. fulgens* and *F. splendens*. It grows to 3-4 metres on a shady wall and flowers for over nine months.

My garden is under designed and over planted. Nonetheless, I rarely look at a special plant and think: 'I have no space left in my garden for you'. Nor do I often say 'this plant is too difficult for me'. I will find a place. I will attempt to grow the impossible plants. I have had many failures and my garden, although full of good plants, is still a graveyard for many killed specimens and hopes.

Still it is my joy, my pastime, my own little inconsequential work of art, and, most of the time, it pleases me.

Garden Notebook

Suggestions for growing tender plants:

Brugmansia sanguinea: Previously known as *Datura sanguinea*, this Brazilian native is poisonous in leaf and flower. In spring, plant it in a sheltered spot once danger of frost is over so that plant can get good growth over summer and autumn. In late autumn cut back some of the branches and cover with fleece for the first few winters. Established plants can take several degrees of frost.

Walls covered with trellis are very useful for growing tender climbers such as Fuchsia 'Gesneriana'. In winter fleece can be pinned over the plant by using clothes pegs to secure it to the trellis.

Hedychium forrestii is generally regarded as the hardiest of the gingers. As an additional protection against frost in winter, cover it with a generous mulch of compost.

I like to use 'a belt and braces approach' when experimenting with tender plants. When I bought *Polygala myrtifolia* in the house plant section of a nursery, I brought it home, propagated it and then planted it out. This great plant carries flowers on every day of the year and is well worth trying in a warm part of the garden, preferably near the house and not in a frost pocket.

Dieramas, popularly known as Angel's Fishing Rods are very beautiful plants that need a well-drained spot in full sun with no competition from neighbours. The seed heads are very attractive and should be left on the plant so that, hopefully, they will spread themselves around the garden.

Rosa 'Perle d'Or' is an easy, adaptable plant with leaves that don't seem to suffer from blackspot or rust. It grows to about a metre in height and, if deadheaded regularly, it will flower for many months in summer. This is the rose that the late great rosarian Graham Stuart Thomas wore as a buttonhole.

very useful for softening concrete slabs on a patio or for growing in old walls. Although it seeds itself generously, it is not a difficult plant to control. It will flower all year long but benefits from being cut back (with a hedge clippers) each spring.

My NCCPG
National Plant Collection
of Lathyrus
by Sylvia M. Norton

Erigeron karvinskianus (The Mexican Daisy) is a pretty little daisy that is

T he genus is an interesting one with over 150 species, yet most people
will know of only one and that is *Lathyrus odoratus*, known at first as
the sweet-scented pea and now as the sweet pea. This purple and maroon
highly scented pea is a great favourite with everyone though it is now the
many cultivars which have been bred from this original that are in great
demand today for gardens and for floristry. Lathyrus was formerly in the family
Leguminosae now Fabaceae and in the subfamily Papilionoidae which means
'like butterflies'. The flowers look very fragile but are really quite sturdy and
range from a few millimetres to almost 4 centimetres across. The colours cover
the full spectrum from white through cream, yellow, gingery-orange, pink,
purple and blue. There are annuals and perennials, climbers, herbaceous and
ground coverers. There are also a few very strange species.

Lathyrus odoratus first described as growing in Sicily, was a purple and blue
bicolour with a very strong scent. Seeds of this annual climber first reached
this country in 1697. The flowers were smaller than we expect today and with
only two flowers per stem. There are now several forms of this species with a
variety of names including Quito, Matucana, Wild Pea and Mediterranean pea
but all have the instantly recognisable strong perfume which can surround you
on a warm, humid day. A cultivar known as 'Painted Lady' with a rich pink
standard and white wings was found in the 19th century and by the end of that
century there were dozens of cultivars known collectively as Grandiflora types.

Herbaceous Perennials
The very first to flower, beginning as early as March if the weather is fair
is *Lathyrus vernus*, the Spring Pea. This herbaceous perennial forms rounded
clumps; the flowers are held well above the emerging leaves welcoming the
spring and defying most that capricious weather can bring. There are 2-4 pairs
of oval leaflets on each stem and 4-8 small pea flowers in purples, pinks, blues
and near whites. When the flowers fade the leaves make a taller mound of
fresh green. I grow them under shrub roses where they benefit from the shade

cover when the roses are in full bloom.

There are several of these herbaceous species, none of which climbs but range in height from 30-90 centimetres. The next to flower is *L. venetus*. This has smaller flowers but many more on each stem, red/purple with darker veins. They have seeded here and made a lovely patch. *L. niger* so named because the whole plant turns black as it dies, is much taller at 90-100 centimetres. Again the purple veined flowers are small but with up to fifteen on each stem. The whole plant makes a pretty fountain shape with sprays of flowers in the axils of the leaves.

Lathyrus 'Painted Lady' courtesy of Deborah Begley

About similar height but with sprays of up to twenty-five larger flowers in golden yellow fading to gingery orange is *L. aureus*. This is happy in shade and really glows when in full flower: a great asset to any garden. Another creamy yellow species is *Lathyrus davidii*. Named after Pere David, it comes from China and Japan. It is taller than *L. aureus*, the leaves more fleshy and the spikes longer. I have not been able to keep it many years in my heavy clay soil; it dislikes cold, wet feet but is worth persevering with.

There are several other herbaceous species, some annuals as well as the perennials already mentioned. They are not always fully garden worthy but make interesting splashes of colour at the front of borders and when seen growing en masse in their native habitat are a great joy.

Perennial Climbers
The perennial climbers contain some of the more vigorous species.
Now establishing itself along motorways and railway lines here is the so-called everlasting pea *Lathyrus latifolius* flowering from June-October. This is a strong grower with winged stems, strong tendrils and more than ten magenta flowers on each stem. There is also a pretty pale pink form which is my favourite and a striking white form. They will climb to two metres and more and will clothe a fence or wall providing there is something to cling to.

Gertrude Jekyll used to plant the white form behind spring flowering shrubs and allow it to cover the shrub thus extending the flowering season. I have them round my fruit cage but canes or wigwams at the back of borders would produce a column of flower. The white form *L. latifolius* 'Albus' climbs through a cotoneaster on my garage wall. *L. rotundifolius* comes into flower a little earlier and is not quite so tall but covered in brick pink flowers for several weeks. The extra rain and warmth this year has prolonged the flowering season.

Perhaps this is the secret, I am always finding new things about these lovely plants. These perennial climbers make a great deal of top growth each year forming steadily increasing rootstocks. There are however some with invasive running roots. *L. grandiflorus* has the largest flowers in crimson and purple about 4 centimetres across but with a very invasive root system. I am very fond of it and when in full flower (June-July) it is a magnificent sight but do not plant it unless you have room for it to spread. *L. tuberosus* also has invasive roots. I have planted it under my old shrub roses where it scrambles happily up through them and out to the grass where of course it gets cut off. The flowers are the same rich rose pink as *Rosa* 'De Rescht' and to see it climbing through the roses and waving cheekily over the top is a delight. Two climbing perennials which deserve to be better known are *L. heterophyllus* and *L. cirrhosus*. These do not reach more than 90 centimetres and have green tinged pink flowers. Good value if you have only a small space.

Climbing Annuals

Three climbing annuals that are well worth growing are *L. tingitanus* the Tangier pea, *L. chloranthus* and *L. sativus*. The Tangier pea is a rich purple crimson with long narrow leaflets, the second has lime green flowers and *L. sativus* is that beautiful electric blue with a red splodge in the centre. If you have a meadow then *L. pratensis*, a yellow flowered perennial will twine itself happily up the long grass stems. *L. nissolia* which looks like grass until you see the small red flowers is an annual as is *L. aphaca* with small yellow flowers above strange shield shaped stipules which take the place of leaves. This will seed itself around very happily but being an annual is quite easy to get rid of.

The species mentioned cover a wide range of countries and habitats but all in the old world, Europe and Asia. The Americas have their own quite separate group of endemic species but although many of the old world plants have been successfully introduced into both north and south America, none from those countries has been found in the wild in Europe or Asia. I grow *L. nervosus*, *L. pubescens* and one or two others from South America and I know they have been grown for a short period of time outdoors in Britian but I keep them in pots and give them shelter in the winter. Three North American species grow happily here but they too need winter protection.

Characteristics

The leaves are as varied as the flowers, with one or many pairs of leaflets. Some are narrow and lance shaped, others round or oblong and almost as wide as long. Many are rather heavy while others are dainty and show off their flowers to perfection. The seed pods show a tremendous variation in size, shape and form and are often a main identifying feature. Seeds are just as variable.

Propagation

Propagation by seed is easy. The species do not cross which is a blessing when growing several in a garden. Seed is ripe if the pods rattle when tapped. I rub the seeds between sandpaper, soak them overnight and sow the annuals ten to a 7 centimetre pot. Sow in the autumn for an early crop or in early spring as long as wet and cold are not a problem. They can also be sown directly into the ground. I have mice, voles and pigeons so I prefer to sow in pots and plant out in May. Then I have more control of them.

As with sweet peas, when they have attained four pairs of true leaflets, pinch out the tips to encourage side shoots and therefore the chance of more flowers. They are fully hardy but do not plant out if there is a risk of frost. Many will self seed and I have fair success, but if mild early spring weather is interrupted by frost you could lose them. I prick out the perennial seedlings when they have two or three pairs of true leaves into 7 centimetre pots.

Pests and Diseases

Greenfly and red spider mite can be a problem if plants are kept under cover. Rabbits love the young shoots. Some are prone to mildew and although I have tried many preparations I am not as persistent as the mildew.

I took early retirement from teaching and after making my new garden look as lovely as possible I wanted a new focus. I had recently heard of the National Council for the Conservation of Plants and Gardens, was already growing sweet peas and wondered about a National Collection. My parents were very keen gardeners and though none of us had much botanical knowledge we often rehearsed the few names we knew. I knew for instance that sweet peas were in the genus *Lathyrus* but not much more. Early enquiries found about forty species and with access to twenty, I thought a National Collection would be a good idea. It was rather a shock to find on deeper research that there were in fact one hundred and sixty four species world wide. Nothing ventured, nothing gained and with the help of the Cambridgeshire NCCPG Group members I started to gather seeds and plants from as many sources as possible and National Collection status was granted in 1991. I felt very honoured indeed to be awarded NCCPG's Brickell Award for excellence in cultivated plant conservation in 2005.

What started as a hobby has turned into a compulsion and given me much pleasure as well as increasing my knowledge of botany and gaining me many friends in this country and abroad.

An Encounter with a Garden Eccentric

by Val Dennison

I truly believe that it is in 'gardening' that one will find the majority of the eccentrics of this world. This has been my experience over the period of my interest in gardening matters. It never fails to astonish me just how many gardeners and plants-people manage to 'plough their own furrow', 'do their own thing,' live their obsessions in fact.

Do plants and gardens themselves engender this obsessive and eccentric trait or is it the eccentric nature itself that is drawn to plants and gardens? Who knows, but I have certainly met a number of amazing individuals involved in the pursuit. People who don't toe the line like the rest of us but who are determined to be themselves - in spite of the rest of us. Below is an example of one such encounter with a lady who grew cacti and succulents (and mice) to perfection.

The elderly woman came into view. She was accompanied by what appeared to be a train, a swath of movement that swept from side to side and around her as she hove towards the gate. The swirl of movement was yapping furiously and turned out to be a dozen or so young Boxer puppies. Where she went, they went. With some trepidation we entered the yard and were instantly and equally enveloped in puppy dogs. Oblivious to the boisterous attention of the animals, she lead us towards to the dilapidated glass house that housed the succulents we had come to see. Noting the neglected state of the place, we weren't expecting much and wondered if the journey to purchase 'fat' plants was going to be worth the effort and subsequently the dry cleaning costs necessary to remove the canine slobber from our clothes.

The place housing our interest was at the far end of a series of shredded, flapping, one-time plastic tunnels and old wooden sheds. It was one of these sheds that housed the parrot...

The Macaw patrolled a perch, on a stand, placed en route to the succulent house. It was clear that the beast understood the job description - that it had to defend 'the pass' at all costs and hence to attack all visitors with the energy and dedication of a maniac.

This it proceeded to do (add the cost of repair of jacket sleeve to list). Feeling that we were characters accompanying Christian in John Bunyan's epic, we wondered what other hazards were in store, prior to reaching the Celestial City of turgid, fat, greenness.

The mouse shed was interesting. Here were fifty or more little boxes with grills, on a wall, filled with mice. Rare and pedigree mice to be sure but mice all the same. The little squeaking inmates added their dusty, agitated presence to that of the rest of the menagerie as we squeezed past them to the succulent house.

We were not ready for the awesome sight of fully-grown Agaves and columnar cacti that met our gaze in the high, rickety glass house. These were the show plants that had won gold medals and wowed visitors at countless flower show events but were now too big and heavy and established, for an elderly lady to manage. They were pushing through the roof, spilling across the staging and the beds. The little woman shrank against her monster children. Yes, there was a son who worked and wasn't always around anyway and he wasn't interested in plants. So these mighty twisting and stripy monsters were left to wander and age, in the space of the old greenhouse. 'Wasn't Kew interested in taking them?' I asked her. 'Surely such a wonderful collection…'

'No, there was no interest' she replied. She really wanted to sell us the monster *Echinocactus grusonii*, the round pouffe shaped, but lethally spiky, 'mother in law's cushion' or 'golden barrel cactus'. It had been to all the shows, but was now too gross for moving.

How could we not take this magnificent creature off her hands? It was a couple of hours later that we found ourselves once more outside the gate. Leaving the woman and the dogs shuffling and swaying back towards the buildings, we staggered toward the car with the golden barrel cactus.

It took a while for the dry cleaning to return, the sleeves to be sewn and the cactus wounds to heal.

The epilogue

We carefully tended the cactus, delighting in its golden girth. Until a year or so later, when it appeared to be getting smaller. On inspection and a poke with a stick, it became all style and no content – it collapsed into a deflated, thorny hide and lay folded in on itself, on top of the pot. We had over-watered it during the winter months and it had reacted by dying.

What happened to the cactus lady, her parrot, her dogs and her mice? I have no idea.

The National Botanic Gardens of Ireland

*Building on their history
to ensure a relevant future*
by Peter Wyse Jackson

Over the last few decades, botanic gardens throughout the world have undergone a remarkable transformation. As the greatest repositories of living plant collections worldwide, their importance and roles are so much better understood and appreciated by increasingly wide audiences and many botanic gardens have been reinvigorated and rejuvenated to undertake a wide range of new tasks, particularly in education and plant conservation. Worldwide – botanic gardens receive more than 200 million visitors and grow over 100,000 plant species (probably about one quarter of the plants of the world are included in their collections) – what Noah did for animals, botanic gardens are now doing for plants. As well as that, the contribution of botanic gardens to cultural development, to economic progress and commercial expansion has been of very great significance to many countries throughout the world over the last four centuries since the first botanic garden was created.

In Ireland, the transformation and restoration of the National Botanic Gardens at Glasnevin represents a fine example of the new roles and recognition of important historic botanic gardens. The developments at Glasnevin not only include such high-profile projects as the restoration of the Curvilinear Glasshouse range and the Great Palm House by the Office of Public Works, but also the construction of a fine new Visitor and Education Centre, the restoration of the Director's Residence (the oldest building in the Gardens) and an excellent building to house the National Herbarium, the Gardens' library and art collection and a small laboratory.

The Curvilinear Range of Glasshouses, built from 1843-1869, are historic buildings in the Gardens of outstanding architectural importance. Designed by Richard Turner and largely built by him they are of cast and wrought iron construction. In the early 1990s they were badly dilapidated and a complete and faithful restoration was undertaken by the Office of Public Works to bring them back to their former glory. In 1884 the Great Palm House of the National Botanic Gardens was built. It too had become derelict before a major restoration by the Office of Public Works was completed in 2004. Today the glasshouse contains an internationally important orchid

collection and diverse tropical and succulent plants from around the world.
A particular focus on plants of Central America is included, developed in
collaboration with the Belize Botanic Gardens. As part of this redevelopment,
in 2005, a traditional Maya Rainforest House was built in the Palm House, a
centrepiece for new educational programmes. The house was inaugurated by
former Taoiseach, Mr Bertie Ahern T.D.

The history of the National Botanic Gardens is well known. They were
established in 1795, founded by the (Royal) Dublin Society, with the support
of funds from the Irish Parliament. Between 1790–1795 the Irish Parliament
provided £2,200, and £500 was given by the Dublin Society to establish the
Gardens for which the former country estate of Thomas Tickell was purchased.
Tickell was a minor English poet in the early 1700s who came to Ireland as an
assistant to the statesman, writer and poet Joseph Addison who was Secretary
to the Lord Lieutenant of Ireland. The oldest part of the Garden remains a Yew
walk (*Taxus baccata*) planted in the 1740s, called Addison Walk, possibly named
by Tickell in memory of his friend and mentor. Following its creation, the
Gardens were opened to the general public in 1800 – 1801. Shortly afterwards
this was changed and they were open to non-members of the Dublin Society
by ticket only. Apparently *'idle persons and particularly children' had got into the
Gardens and 'done considerable mischief'*. Non-members had to be accompanied
around the Gardens by the Head Gardener personally. Today the Gardens are
open to the public, free of charge, every day except Christmas Day.
Idle persons and particularly children are very welcome! In 1877 the Gardens
were transferred by the Royal Dublin Society, to the State (under the care of the
Dept of Agriculture). In 1992 they were moved to become a part of the Office
of Public Works (OPW) (Heritage Services) which remains their parent body.

Botanic gardens are complex institutions however. It is not even easy to
define what is a botanic garden. What makes a botanic garden different from
any public park, recreation area or indeed from our own private gardens?
It is not an easy question to answer and until recently there has not been a
widely accepted definition of a botanic garden available. In the 1960s one

source defined them as 'gardens which are open to the public and the plants are labelled' – fine as far as it goes. But what about their roles as centres for education, amenity and recreation, biodiversity conservation, scientific research, horticulture, training, tourism, information management and other activities? It is actually the complex interactions and applications of this diversity of roles and activities that makes botanic gardens unique. The recent definition of a botanic garden adopted by Botanic Gardens Conservation International – *'botanic gardens are institutions holding documented collections of living plants for the purposes of scientific research, conservation, display and education'* – illustrates the multipurpose functions of botanic gardens.

I have often been asked 'how many botanic gardens are there in the world?', a question which is difficult to answer satisfactorily – partly because it is not always easy to define whether a particular garden is 'botanic' or not, but mainly because, remarkably, there are so many new botanic gardens being created throughout the world that whenever I give a figure it is almost immediately out of date. Almost weekly I hear of a new botanic garden being planned or established somewhere in the world. Today we know of over 2,500 institutions defined as botanic gardens, in 153 countries. More than half of these botanic gardens have been created over the last fifty years.

In Europe, the first botanic gardens to be founded were medicinal or physic gardens whose primary function was to provide material and facilities for students in university faculties of medicine in Ireland, Italy, France, Switzerland, the Netherlands, the UK and other countries. For example, the oldest botanic garden in Ireland, the Trinity College Botanic Garden was founded in 1687, as a source of plant material for medical teaching in the College. Over time many of these gardens adopted wider roles in scientific research, particularly in plant classification and taxonomic botany, roles which continue up to the present day. In other parts of the world, earlier gardens which could claim to be 'botanic' were created in previous civilizations, such as China, pre-Hispanic Mexico and the Arab world, but we still have too little knowledge of how they function to be sure whether any can be described as the first true botanic gardens.

What is generally regarded as the first ever botanic garden was the medicinal garden established at Pisa in 1543. It was followed closely by Padua (1545) (which still survives today in its original form), Florence (1545) and Bologna (1547). Then came Zurich (1560), Leiden (1577), Leipzig (1579), Paris (1597), Montpellier (1598), Oxford (1621), Uppsala (1655), Edinburgh (1670), Berlin (1679) and Amsterdam (1682). All of these botanic gardens exist to today, most of them in their original locations. From these early beginnings many of the major European botanic gardens have evolved to become the great institutions they are today, representing 'classic' botanic gardens with a broad range of activities in horticulture, horticultural training, research (particularly in taxonomy – with associated herbaria and laboratories), public amenity and education. This botanic garden model has been widely adopted in other countries mainly as national institutions.

The development of early tropical botanic gardens was more motivated by considerations of trade and commerce than by science for its own sake. European colonial powers, particularly Britain, the Netherlands, and to a lesser extent Germany, Belgium, Spain and Portugal, established important tropical botanic gardens in their colonies in Africa, the Caribbean, India, South–East Asia and South America in the 18th and 19th centuries. The first botanic garden to be founded in the tropics was the Pamplemousses garden in the Indian Ocean island of Mauritius, founded in 1729 (now the Sir Seewoosagur Ramgoolam Botanic Garden). It was initially established to provide fresh fruit and vegetables for the colony and to provide provisions for ships calling at the nearly port of St Louis. Through the Garden many economic plants were introduced, such as sugarcane and spice plants, which became the basis of the island's economy. Many of the earliest tropical botanic gardens had similar origins through which economically useful plants were introduced, such as breadfruit, cinchona, cloves, cocoa, coffee, oil palm and rubber, often associated with one of the major European gardens such as Amsterdam and Kew. Notable amongst these early tropical gardens, many of which still thrive today, are St Vincent (1765); St Denis, Réunion Island (1765); Calcutta, India (1787);

Rio de Janeiro, Brazil (1808); Sydney (1816) and Hobart (1818), Australia; Bogor, Indonesia (1817); Peradeniya, Sri Lanka (1821); Durban, South Africa (1849); Singapore (1859) and Bath (1779), Castleton (1859), Cinchona (1868) and Kingston (1872), Jamaica.

In temperate regions a large number of urban municipal botanic gardens were founded in the 19th and 20th centuries. In the 20th century, such gardens were a particular feature in the United States, Australia and New Zealand. Many of these gardens did not develop major scientific facilities but there are notable exceptions to this, such as Missouri Botanical Garden, which was founded in 1859, the first botanic garden in the United States. Another exception was the Palmengarten in Frankfurt, Germany, founded in 1869. Most of these municipal botanic gardens developed significant activities in horticulture, building and maintaining major documented plant collections.

In the countries of the former Soviet Union, the earliest botanic gardens are in Russia – the Apothecaries Garden of Moscow State University was created in 1706 and the botanic gardens of the Komarov Institute in St Petersburg, was founded in 1713 - but many of the 100+ botanic gardens have been created within the last fifty years, mainly to act as centres for botanical research and plant introduction and generally associated with their national academy of science and universities. In China, more than 100 botanic gardens have been created in the last twenty years, mainly to support horticulture, research, native plant conservation, local education and as a place for public relaxation.

In the last twenty to thirty years there has been a renaissance in botanic gardens worldwide, largely as a result of the developing concern for biodiversity loss and the need for many more institutions to become active in plant resources conservation. There has also been a corresponding rise in botanic garden involvement in research and conservation of the floras of the regions or countries in which they are situated. In some countries, most notably in Australia, Brazil, Colombia, India, Mexico and others, a recent trend has been the creation of local or community botanic gardens. These are often relatively modest institutions developed and managed by community groups to suit a variety of local needs, for plant conservation (such as of medicinal plants in several developing countries), environmental education and public amenity. The collections of these gardens are predominantly made up of native species and often constituted to support or complement nearby efforts made to conserve plants in their natural habitats, in nature reserves and national parks.

The National Botanic Gardens at Glasnevin are therefore extremely well placed to contribute effectively to life in Ireland, as well as to be a internationally recognised leader amongst botanic gardens. The collections of the Gardens are of considerable international importance and include over 17,000 species and varieties in cultivation. The Gardens receive over half a million visitors a year and are one of Dublin and Ireland's major visitor attractions, beloved by residents and tourists alike. Plant conservation has become a major focus of the Gardens' work and the collections currently include over 400 rare or endangered species from around the world. The Irish National Herbarium in the Gardens with three quarters of a million preserved plant specimens, is an important scientific reference collection for botanical research and the Library is an internationally significant treasure-house of botanical literature, containing over 50,000 volumes and 3,500 botanical art works.

Over the coming years major plans have been put in place to continue to enhance and expand the Gardens roles and facilities. These will include the restoration of the historic Cactus and Succulent House (1900) and Aquatic House (1853) as well as the redevelopment of a new more suitable Fern House. A new area of the Garden was redeveloped over the last two years and opened to the public for the first time in 2008, to demonstrate and display fruit and vegetable gardening, managed according to organic principles. New educational projects include a particular focus on sustainability – recycling, environmentally-friendly gardening, composting, reducing waste and energy consumption and biodiversity conservation. A major new native plant conservation area is being planned including a range of rare or endangered Irish plant species. Important new plant collections from various parts of the world, notably from China, Russia and Latin America have been added, gathered during scientific expeditions undertaken by staff over the last few years. In 1995 the National Botanic Gardens took over the management of the Kilmacurragh Arboretum in Kilbride, Co. Wicklow. It is being restored and developed as the Garden's satellite south of Dublin and increasingly welcomes thousands of new visitors each year.

The 21st century will be an exciting and important time for the National Botanic Gardens and indeed for all botanic gardens worldwide when they will face increasingly challenging tasks. We now recognise that there is a desperately urgent extinction crisis facing the world's biodiversity. Over the coming century it is estimated that up to two-thirds of the world's plants will become threatened in the wild and the situation can be even worse if the expected impacts of climate change cause the loss of many wild plant habitats. Botanic gardens are responding with the development of new plant conservation initiatives throughout the world as well as embracing the need to raise public concern for plants and the environment. For all of us working at the National Botanic Gardens, it is very rewarding to be part of an institution that is increasingly recognized in Ireland and internationally for its importance and for its essential and multiple roles.

Unusual Magnolias

by Stephen Redden

As a young nurseryman I had always admired the flowering *Magnolia 'soulangiana'* growing on the Ennis Rd. in Limerick. With a bit of research I found out that *Magnolia soulangiana* was bred by a French military man in Napoleons army! His name was Chevalier Etainne Soulange-Bodin and this magnolia became the most celebrated magnolia in horticulture.

Whilst on holiday in Wales in 1998 I visited Hay-on-Wye, the 'Town of Books' and there I purchased my first book on Magnolias by the curator of Wisley, (The Royal Horticultural Society's garden in Surrey.) Jim M. Gardener, and there started my love affair with magnolias. Since opening Hillberry Garden Centre in County Limerick in 2000 I have indulged my passion for magnolias by purchasing as many varieties as I could and persuading my customers that everyone should have a magnolia in their garden.

The name magnolia dates from around 1700 when the French botanist Charles Plumier found one on the island of Martinique in the Indian Ocean and named it it after fellow botanist Pierre Magnol. However it wasn't until the late 18th.century when they were brought back from Asia, that they began to take hold in Europe. One of the reasons being that some of the species could take thirty years to flower! Magnolia is an ancient genus, having evolved before bees appeared. Because of this, the flowers developed to encourage pollination by beetles and as a result the petals or carpels of the flowers are tough and waxy to discourage and prevent damage by eating and crawling insects.

Magnolia 'Big Dude' Seed Head

Cultivation and soil preparation

It goes without saying that the most important task in growing any plant or shrub is to prepare the soil thoroughly, adding a rich bulky organic humus that will be moisture retentive and will cause the soil to be on the slightly acidic side of neutral. The best position for magnolias is a sheltered sunny position to help with blossom development and retention. It is worth bearing in mind the ultimate size of the species to allow adequate room for growing. Too often gardeners plant trees or shrubs in positions that look fine when the plants are young, but then quickly become overwhelmed when the plant reaches maturity, squeezing out other plants or shutting out the light and retarding growth. Magnolias flower from early spring to late summer depending on the variety and they come in all shapes and sizes. In fact there is a magnolia to suit all gardens. The following magnolias are in the Jury hybrids group from New Zealand and are amongst my favourites. *M.* 'Iolanthes'. *M.* 'Atlas'. *M.* 'Athene'. *M.* 'Apollo' and *M.* 'Vulcan'. 'Iolanthes' and 'Atlas' are sisters –'Iolanthes' producing an abundance of large soft, pink bowl shaped blooms, turning paler inside. 'Atlas' has huge flowers at least 30cm wide even on young plants. The flowers appear two or three weeks after its sister but it does need a wind-protected site on account of its huge flowers.

Magnolia 'Apollo' and its sister *M.* 'Vulcan' are again two marvellous varieties from the Jury's stable.

M. 'Apllo' is an exceptionally heavy cropper with a large deep rose pink star like flower. *M.* 'Vulcan' is a smaller tree but has brilliant ruby red flowers.

Two of my favourite yellow magnolias are *Magnolia* 'Butterflies' and *Magnolia* 'Goldstar'. 'Butterflies' is a neat growing upright tree with deep yellow flowers, prominent red anthers, and was a great favourite with Magnolia Society members. *M.* 'Goldstar' is also an upright growing small tree. It has creamy yellow, star-like flowers like the commonly grown *Magnolia stellata*. It has ovate bronzed red leaves turning green as they mature; this hybrid is very hardy and the flowers are very frost tolerant.

Of the soulangiana hybrids I have to say that I have a preference for *M*. 'Big Dude'. It has large fragrant cup shaped reddish purple and white flowers fading to rosepink on the inside of the nine to twelve tepals. It is also very winter hardy and bears striking large red fruit or seeds. One can see from these seed heads, how aptly named the tree is!

Magnolia 'Big Dude'

Magnolia grandiflora 'Charles Dickens' is a broad spreading evergreen variety with very large flowers 30cm. in diameter – lemon scented and beautiful large bright red fruit. *Magnolia* 'Leda' another favourite of mine is also worth the effort. Believed to be a hybrid of *M.cylindica* and *M. campbellii* var. alba this was known as *M*.'White Lips' until 1997 when the name 'Leda' meaning swan was given by Dick van Gelderen when he first saw the flower in the nursery of Mark Bulk of Boskoop in Holland.

It freely produces pure white cup and saucer shaped flowers 23cm. across. *Magnolia macrophylla* subsp.'Ashei' is one of America's rarest magnolias.It is found in N.W. Florida.The leaf size and flowers are smaller than the type, but it is scented and can be pure white or spotted red.A favourable characteristic of this species magnolia is that it flowers in a much shorter time than other species- about three years.

M. 'Raspberry Ice' is a beautiful Gresham hybrid with flowers about 23cm. across, pink - white with violet shading at the base of 12 petals.

It has a shrubby habit, flowering in March.

Magnolia sargentiana var. 'Robusta' (Sargents magnolia) The flowers of this spectacular Chinese species are slightly scented of winter green. The plants flower from a comparatively early age and appear 'like open parachutes of coloured paper'. A mature specimen in full flower with the sheer number of blooms is an amazing sight.

Magnolia 'Starwars' raised again in New Zealand by Oswald Blumhardt is a superb performer. This has to be one of my favourite magnolias. It flowers for 6-8 weeks from mid-March until the end of April. The 28cm. long flowers have 12 rich pink petals borne freely and point in all directions. The pyramidical outline is also quite distinct and has to be seen to be believed. *Magnolia* 'Tino Durio' has huge white cup and saucer shaped pure white flowers with a tiny hint of pink at the base of 12 petals 30cm wide.

This hybrid was named in 1984 for the daughter of Ken Durio of Louisianna.

I have put *Magnolia stellata* 'Water Lily' in my favourite list because it is a very tough variety and stellatas in general are great magnolias to start a collection with: they are easy to grow and put on a fabulous flowering display.

One of my greatest favourites, is the distinct clone 'Water Lily' from England because of its large white flowers and more petals then the type.

The last magnolia I am going to write about is one of my top five favourites. This is *Magnolia* × *wieseneri* a deliciously scented multi-stemmed large shrub. It is a hybrid between two Japanese species, both very good in their own right, *M.hypoleuca* and *M.sieboldii*. The plant is mainly grown for its scent which has been described as medicinal, spicy, aromatic, and like pineapples!

Some more unusual magnolias not mentioned:

Magnolia campbellei ssp. *mollicomata*

Magnolia acuminate 'Blue Opal'

Magnolia sargentiana

Magnolia 'Spectrum'

Magnolia 'Waterlily'

A Decade of Change
at Fota Arboretum & Gardens
by David B. O'Regan

Situated in Cork harbour on what was once an island, Fota Arboretum and Gardens is thought to have been developed from the 1820s on. It all started with the conversion of a grand hunting lodge by John Smith-Barry to a permanent residence. The famous Morrison architects were employed to carry out the task.

The Smith-Barry family owned large areas of land in Cork, Tipperary and had a large estate in Cheshire in England. The family would have resided in Ireland & England at different times of the year, but probably spent their summers in Fota. During the brief time that they stayed in Fota they made great strides in developing the Arboretum & Gardens. The name Fota comes from the Irish words, 'fód te' meaning warm soil.

From the few records we have, we can see that they were to the fore in the planting of new introductions from North & South America and Asia. In the sheltered mild climate in which Fota is situated, they implemented a policy of growing all these new plants unprotected outdoors. Such was their success that by the end of the 1800s a number of articles were published in horticultural journals extolling the astonishing collection of plants in Fota. Up to the present day, the style of planting within the arboretum is still much commented on. It has been described as 'French Parkland' referring to the open nature of the planting which allows unhindered growth and the benefit to the visitor of unimpeded views of each specimen in all its glory.

Naturally as the property passed from one generation to the next and as the fashions of the times dictated, each generation put their stamp on the Arboretum and Gardens.

It was Lord Barrymore (1845-1925) who lived though the greatest developments of the grounds and whose features are very much an essential part of the style of Fota - he, along with his head gardener, laid out the arboretum in its present style. He also developed the Fernery or Rockery c.1888 with tree ferns received from Dereen Gardens in Co. Kerry. In 1889 he constructed the 'Lady Mary Gates' in honour of his first wife, and they are now the formal entrance to the Pleasure Gardens. Within the Pleasure Gardens he constructed what is called the Italian Garden. Probably, as was fashionable at the time, artefacts were brought home from the continent and the garden was constructed around them. The garden's name is probably derived from the origin of the main feature which is an Italian artefact known as the 'Fouscarrii well head' and reputed to have been constructed in 1455.

His daughter, The Hon. Mrs Bell, (1914-1975) developed the Tennis Court within the Pleasure Gardens. She, I also believe, introduced most of the colour to the Arboretum, which we now have the benefit of today. It was also a feature of her time in Fota that the grounds lost many of the formal designs so typical of the Victorian era. The parterre bedding schemes were the first to go. The old Rose garden was gradually reduced in size; the sundial garden had its entire perennial borders and beds, bar one, removed. This came about because of a gradual reduction in staff, brought on by the rising cost of wages.

On her death in 1975, part of the Estate i.e. Fota Island comprising of 730 acres was bought by UCC. Their primary interest was the agricultural land, which would be utilised by their Agriculture & Food Science Dept.

A Decade of Change 1996-2006

Since my appointment as head gardener at Fota Arboretum & Gardens, my functions and responsibilities have been varied, challenging and inspiring. For a number of years, prior to my arrival, the importance of the gardens as a horticultural gem was overshadowed by the success of Fota Wildlife Park. The gardens had also suffered under the management of a university agricultural department who, while endeavouring to develop the amenity, were really only maintaining it in a state of limbo. Unfortunately, in some circumstances, they physically destroyed some of the classical features of the gardens.

As the state had agreed to take over the arboretum & gardens, just prior to my appointment, there was a positive air of optimism amongst the staff. Coincidentally the age profile of the staff was greatly lowered around this time due to the recruitment of additional staff.

I wasn't in Fota long when one of the most significant and daunting tasks, as I then thought, had to be faced. This was the provision of guided tours, by me, to lay and specialist groups. But over time it has become a function which I enjoy and even look forward to. Very often it is the main method by which I receive feedback from the general visitor as to their impressions of our completed restoration projects and also their overview of the general appearance of the grounds.

As a follow on from this and my ability to carry out this function adequately, I have been asked to talk on radio, give press interviews, and frequently speak to garden clubs throughout the country, north and south. I have also made contributions to horticultural publications.

Thankfully, with some foresight, I personally and at my own expense started to record on slide - plants and places before we started to redevelop the grounds. The importance of this was brought home when we were severely hit by a storm and lost a sizeable number of the older trees.

When I arrived in Fota the grounds could be divided into four main areas:

Area 1:	Arboretum
Area 2:	Pleasure Gardens
Area 3:	Old Fruit & Veg. Garden
Area 4:	Glasshouses

Area 1

The Arboretum was severely depleted due to poor planning, work practices, storm damage and would require considerable planting to halt the regression. While the first year was very much a case of getting to know the arboretum, there was an immediate start made on bringing sections of it back under our control. This entailed the removal of large sections of *Prunus laurocerasus* that were of little benefit to the arboretum and the area cleared could be more appropriately utilised. I also set about lifting and transplanting trees within the arboretum for which little thought had been given to their eventual impact on surrounding plants. Over the years I have added a large number of trees and shrubs to the collection while always remaining conscious of its style of planting.

By means of regular inspection, problems are quickly noted and remedial action taken where appropriate. It has to be said that in recent years some of the problems which are occurring are a cause for serious concern. Trees and shrubs which are young, vigorous and appear to be on their way to a full life are suddenly, very often within months, dying off with no apparent reason. Other more hardy trees with a reputation for longevity are again rapidly succumbing to unknown causes. If this is a result of global warming then it is a worrying trend for the future!

Area 2

During the late '70s, the Pleasure Garden was almost completely stripped of its remaining features and only the old herbaceous border which survived gave a small indication of its former glory. By interviewing the semi-retired previous head gardener I was able to glean an impression of what the borders contained, and their colour scheme. I used this as a template in my restoration of same.

After some additional investigation and discussion with previous staff, I was able to replant sections of the yew hedging, which had been removed in the late '70s. They were so important to the subdivision of the pleasure gardens and consequently the new plantings have been an outstanding success.

The remaining original Yew hedges were unmanageable and unsightly, so a programme of regeneration was initiated from day one. This has and will be an ongoing project over a number of years. Work already completed has been very successful.

One other feature, which had been sadly neglected over time, was a Wisteria. While flowering was profuse it had become rooted to the top of its supporting wall and was completely out of control. It was also infected with ivy and bindweed. After cutting it down to ground, any viable stems that could be

utilised were reattached to a reconditioned wiring of the wall. As a result
of programmed pruning the effect of its original creation is becoming
an annual display.

In recent years a sub section called the Italian Garden has been
reconstructed by OPW architects. Regular site meetings allowed me an
understanding of the project and also help us achieve an accurate interpretation.
The garden staff completed the soft landscaping and I now plan and plant a bi-
annual display of bedding within the garden.

Area 3

While used as a fruit and vegetable garden for many decades, the university
used it for a few years to trial crops but in the early '90s it was cleaned up and
put down to grass.

Immediately on my arrival it was agreed with my line manager that this
garden would primarily feature roses in the main quads. Once the layout was
approved I set about selecting varieties and deciding on a colour scheme.
For added interest I developed themed borders on the four surrounding walls.
These are Monocots 2, Central/South American and a Shade border. In three
of these borders I also incorporated a collection of Irish bred daffodils, which
required very careful planning within a mixed border setting.

As the garden has matured and developed so has the need for regular
reassessment, lifting, dividing, replanting and the addition of new features
where appropriate. In order to procure the vast number of plants to fill such
large borders a number of sources have been tapped.

The National Botanic Gardens set us on our way by providing a wide
range of plants for the borders, with varying degrees of hardiness. Other gardens,
both private and public from home and abroad contributed. Garden clubs also
made donations. Some purchases were also made, but a large number of plants
were grown from seed.

Area 4

In order to develop and protect these young plants some of the old pit houses were rescued from beneath the mass of briars and other weeds that engulfed them. A new roof and capillary bed was then installed. As a result, a large range of new plants were grown which were subsequently transferred to the arboretum or gardens as appropriate.

In conclusion my work at Fota has been varied, challenging, rewarding and educational. For the future it will, I'm sure, allow further development of it and me, in equal measure.

Historic References:
Dúchas *Fota Arboretum & Gardens,* Visitors' Guide
Fota House, The Irish Heritage Series No 44, 1984
Fota House & Gardens, Fota Trust 2002
The Garden Nov 27th 1875,
The Gardeners Chronicle July 2nd 1940

Looking Back
and Forward
by Brian Cross

Memories came flooding back today when a Dutch lady paid a return visit after 20 years to the garden. 'Oh', she said in broken English, 'the garden is so beautiful'. She had so many lovely comments, and remembered Mrs Cross senior with a welcoming smile.

My own first memories of gardening at Lakemount included growing Sweet William for my grandmother and helping Tom, our old gardener who treated the garden as his own (how dare we pick the peas or cut the grass!) He was in his late seventies wearing a three piece suit and soft hat which he took off when my mother appeared, the hat, I mean.

Lakemount in the early 1960s was very different, large areas of lawn with borders on the perimeter which were too far away from the house. We quickly realised that a garden evolves but it must have a good skeleton, so off with us to nurseries gathering and learning as we went.

Fortunately, feature trees including *Acer griseum*, *Pinus montezumae* and the Handkerchief Tree were planted early in our gardening life which are now surrounded by plantings of rhododendrons, azaleas and hydrangeas.

Having visited some gardens in Britain we realised the importance of hard landscaping and features. At this time, we inherited items of garden furniture together with about eight hundred old granite sets and cut stone from Mitchelstown Castle. Our first paved area was surrounding a small pond using my favourite Liscannor stone. Raised beds surround the area and are planted with seasonal interest. On the south side of the house, terraces were constructed using more free standing walls planted with mixed dry loving rock plants. Against the house wall many climbers thrive: abutilons, wisteria, clematis and sweet peas. Tender plants thrive in this 'hot spot': watsonias, cannas, fascicularia and the lovely vallea, producing soft pink flowers in June.

On the boundaries, early plantings of mixed shelter belts protect my treasures. Now, after forty years, trees have matured and produce a canopy under which grow many tender rhododendrons, tree ferns and azaleas. Little did I think that I would be looking up at twelve metre high *Magnolia campbellii* in full flower during March and April at the age of fifty five. A great gardener, Nancy Minchin, encouraged us to turn an old fruit store into a plant house. Here many cold days are spent pottering and training mature standard Fuchsias. This also houses clivias, strelitizas and *Rhododendron dalhousieae* which reminds us of ripple ice cream.

One of my favourite new areas is an orchard. Here mature gnarled apple trees remind me of a Samuel Palmer drawing and grass paths meander through meadow grass. Many snowdrops thrive in this dappled shade while summer time produces a calm green oasis. To end the year, grasses, hydrangeas and acers give a crescendo for autumn interest.

I always longed for a decorative kitchen garden but, alas, even marriage did not give me this. The younger Mrs Cross has taken over this area and turned it into an exciting cottage garden planted with many bulbs and packed with cottage garden perennials.

Well, the past and present have been discussed, the future, well, a matter for discussion. Will we be here in another twenty five years, still pruning and planting or will we be feeding the soil? Who knows? It does not worry me. Enjoy gardening now and plan for the future by planting trees for the next generation.

Pushing the Boundaries

by Hester Forde

Coosheen, situated on the estuary of Cork harbour, has been home to a growing plant collection over the last twenty years. To maintain an interesting and diverse collection of plants at times can be challenging, but not as challenging as our ever changing climate which has been a significant influence on what I grow. Likewise, we are all influenced by gardens which we visit, what plants are fashionable and by great plants people, for me none more so than the great Christopher Lloyd of Great Dixter. It was his plants and plant associations at Dixter that inspired me to push the boundaries of what I could grow. Many of the tender perennials extend the season and associate beautifully with other plants giving an exuberant palate of colour, texture and design in the autumn garden. Increasingly, benign autumns are making some late-flowering salvias and their cultivars a sage choice for late season interest in the garden.

Salvia Leucantha 'Purple Velvet'

I have always had a love affair with salvias and, sadly, find them dismissed by many gardeners because of their late flowering. What a treat they are missing. Realising their garden worthiness, I have tried over the years to seek out as many forms and cultivars of these shrubby perennials as could be found. Arguably, one of the best introductions to date is *Salvia* 'Dyson'. Its sumptuous crimson flowers that mature to a deep pinkish red, held within dark purple calyces and a flowering period from May to late November, has to make this a winner.

Salvia patens 'Guanajuanto' is twice the height of *Salvia patens* the species and has dark blue flowers twice the height of the species and other cultivars. The slender tubers have overwintered in the garden for the last ten years. Plant it with *Canna* 'Red Futurity' and *Dahlia* 'Fata Morgana' and the resulting combination is spectacular. Fine white down covers the stems of *Salvia leucantha* 'Purple Velvet' with purple flowers emerging from purple calyces making it a superb plant for containers. It associates beautifully with cannas, plecanthrus, ergyranthemums, dahlias and verbenas. This salvia I came across at Wollerton Old Hall, Shropshire, which houses the National Salvia Collection.

Salvia splendens 'Burgundy' is classy. New from Bolivia, reaching one metre (but not hardy), it has deep burgundy flowers emerging from purple calyces on long spikes. The foliage is a lovely lime green.

Having received a cutting a few years ago of a salvia called 'Phyllis Fancy' I now believe it to be *Salvia* 'Waverly' which was introduced in California in 1994. It's a plant with an excellent reputation and has become well known. The names of the people who first distributed this plant and the nurseries in which it was grown were not recorded, making it difficult, if not impossible, to determine its origin. Because of Phyllis Fancy's phenomenal vigour it is thought to be of hybrid origin. *Salvia* 'Phyllis Fancy' thrives in a mild climate and has been quite happy outdoors over the last two winters. Reaching to 1.5 metres in both height and width, it is a heavy bloomer from the late spring until the first frosts. The flowers emerge pale lavender and frequently mature white. However, some flowers are completely lavender. Grown as a container subject it needs to be well watered.

A salvia which is much admired by visitors to the garden and, particularly, if they like a smaller and shorter growing salvia is *Salvia* 'Nana' BSWJ10272 which was introduced by Crug Farm Plants. This was a plant found growing on the cold slopes of Volcan de Orizaba, Mexico's highest peak. The leaves are

a dark grey green which are stained purple around the centres and the flowers
are bright blue and white, held on elongated spikes. *Salvia* 'Nana' has been
very happy in a raised bed at Coosheen for the last number of years and begins
flowering around May continuing until the frosts.

    Salvia guaranitica 'Blue Enigma' has been a stalwart in the border for years.
Hailing from woodland margins in subtropical regions of South America,
Salvia 'Blue Enigma' carries pale green, rather shiny leaves, with dark blue
flowers set in green calyx. In the autumn border it associates well with
Crocosmia 'Star of the East', *Hedychium* 'Assam Orange', *Molina* 'Skyracer' and
Lilium speciosum 'Ruburm'.

Agapanthus 'Black Magic'

I have a particular affinity with the genus gladiolus, a very large genus, perhaps
as many as 150 species. A widespread genus, mainly African but also with
several species in the Mediterranean region eastwards to the Middle East and
a few in Madagascar and the Mascarene Islands. Gladiolus have erect, often
rather tough and strongly ribbed sword shaped leaves with spikes of irregular
shaped flowers and characteristically with a hooded upper segment, a curved
tube and often with contrasting markings on the three lower segments.

    I grow gladiolus mainly in a south westerly facing gravel bed with poor gritty soil where they seem to be happy and also in a raised bed in my back garden which faces south and has lots of grit added. Both areas are top dressed with 6 cm of gravel. *Gladiolus papilio* which hails from the Eastern Cape in South Africa is a vigorous species and very hardy and has given rise to many good hybrids. One of these is *Gladiolus papilio* 'Ruby'. Astonishing ruby red flowers which nod and reach a height of over a metre makes it an excellent contribution to the garden. Growing with cannas, dahlias, salvias and *Cosmos peucedanifolius* all create an exotic feel. A similar hybrid is *Gladiolus papilio* 'David Hills' with peach red, nodding flowers. *Gladiolus* 'Flevo Cosmic', which

Agapanthus 'Merchant's Cobalt'

flowers in August, always reminds me of rhubarb and custard because of it's colouring. Slightly later in the season is *Gladiolus garneiri* from Madagascar which appears to be perfectly hardy. It carries large salmon pink flowers on 75cm stems in August and early September. Other summer flowering gladiolus which flower well at Coosheen are *Gladiolus cardinalis*, the waterfall gladiolus, which has amazing cardinal red flowers with white flashes. Flowering from June to August on 70cm stems it originates in the Drakensberg and is thought to be virtually extinct now in the wild. At the other end of the season is *Gladiolus* 'Huttonii', a delicate classically shaped orange with pink gladiolus

flowers. It flowers at Coosheen from February to March on 60cm stems.
The genus gladiolus are a very worthwhile corm for the gardener who likes to
try something different.

Cannas are a perfect compliment to salvias and gladiolus. Their voluptuous
flowers and handsome leaves exude glamour. Flowering from July until the end
of the gardening year, this sculpture like feature is a must for the exotic garden.
Canna 'Black Knight' has large, floppy, deep crimson flowers with reflexed petals.
The foliage is a deep bluish purple and is a perfect foil to the red flowers on
stems up to two metres in height. Quite distinct from most other cannas is
'Panache'. It carries large open trusses of small, delicately pale apricot flowers,
shaded strawberry-pink, giving a delicate spidery effect. The leaves are large
and upright which are bluish in colour on two metre stems. Of all the cannas
I grow, my favourite has to be *Canna* 'Red Futurity'. Smaller in stature
and at one metre in height it is ideal for containers and beds. It has intense,
medium sized crimson flowers over rich dark-chocolate foliage. It is perhaps
the darkest canna of all and is the best of an American series of dark cannas.
Then, in total contrast, is *Canna striata* syn. 'Bengal Tiger', with pale green leaves
conspicuously striped with gold. Stems and leaf edges have a plum colouring
and the flowers are large and strident orange. *Canna striata* grows to 1.5 metres.
A new introduction is *Canna* 'Sunset' with leaves blacker than Australia and
big red flowers which are slightly orange tinted. It is a beauty. Its foliage and
leaf formation is what makes it stand out from other cannas. All cannas blend
effortlessly in the late-season garden with miscanthus, molinia, dahlias and
other late flowering perennials.

Agapanthus - the African Lily - are elegant and free flowering plants for
a sunny border or a container that bring an ever growing range of blue and
white hues to the garden at Coosheen. In recent years a huge number of
cultivars have been introduced some of which are well worth growing for the
intensity of their colour. *Agapanthus* 'Mood Indigo', a dark blue inapertus, is a
superb introduction and a late flowerer from late August to mid September.
A wonderful large flowered form of agapanthus with powder-blue flowers, got

originally from Gary Dunlop in County Down, is grown in the shelter of the east wall of the house. Another late flowerer *Agapanthus* 'Loch Hope' combines beautifully with *Monarda* 'Mowhawk' and *Persicaria* 'Red Dragon'. *Agapanthus* 'Loch Hope' has very large heads of good dark blue flowers with bluer mid stripes. It grows up to two metres.

Agapanthus 'Black Panther', raised in Australia and now widely grown, has blue/black buds opening out into heads of violet above dark stems of 110cm. *Agapanthus* 'Black Magic' says it all. This is the nearest I've ever seen to having completely black buds opening to a very dark blue flower which flowers in mid season. On a recent trip to Devon and Cornwall I came across *Agapanthus* 'Merchant's Cobalt' grown beautifully with *Chionochloa rubra* which was the perfect foil for the intensely navy blue flowers.

Growing all of the aforementioned plants over the years has been most rewarding. I am forever in pursuit of new plants and better cultivars and wanting to extend the growing boundaries as far as possible.

From Field to Woodland

by Susan Tindall

In 1973 I moved, along with my husband and two small sons, to Ballynahinch in Co. Down. We originally came to Northern Ireland in 1968 from Newcastle upon Tyne. Our first garden in Comber, Co. Down was no bigger than a cabbage patch, and hardly large enough for our sons to have a sand pit. So on our move to Ballynahinch we had 3 acres to play around with. The ground was roughly divided into three lots. The smallest plot was to become the vegetable garden. It had to be cleared of aging laurel, old apple trees, nettles, brambles, and years of accumulated rubbish dumped near an exceedingly large clump of bamboo. The second plot included the house and upper garden, and in the third plot, roughly 1.5 acres, it was decided we would plant trees, rhododendrons and other flowering shrubs, also an area where the boys could play ball games. We decided to call it the Woodland Garden. A friend

Arisaema Candidissimum

once suggested it should be called an arboretum, I decided that to be far too pretentious, and I do appreciate 1.5 acres is not a woodland; it is an area where I can grow shade loving plants under the trees.

The first year our new neighbour and farmer cut the grass and made hay, small oblong bales, not the large rolls of hay and silage one sees around the countryside these days. The following winter and spring of 1974 my husband planted the shelter belt around all the gardens. He would get up very early in the morning before driving to Belfast and plant a few hundred very small trees,

Cypripedium

mainly sitka spruce and scots pine. We should not have planted scots pine as a shelter belt, because as they grew they became very vunerable to wind and gales. One year we had gales on Christmas Eve and forty trees or more came down in the garden; the following year gales took another twenty (not so many trees to be blown down that particular Christmas)!

Once the shelter belt was planted, my husband planted a variety of trees in the woodland garden; quite a few conifers of the more unusual type, plus broad leaf trees. All the trees we planted were only small, less than a metre; some of the trees had been grown by seed. One in particular *Pinus pinea*, has particularly large cones and these are always picked up by visitors to the garden. Other trees we mainly purchased by mail order. We had no trouble with rabbits at this time, so none of trees needed tree guards. We did get the occasional hares racing around and being naughty in the spring time, but, alas, no more hares; they have disappeared altogether.

It took the garden a long time to evolve and it certainly acquired its own micro climate. In the early days we suffered from late frosts and many of the trees suffered as a consequence. We live about 100 metres above sea level and it is in a frost pocket.

Planting up the garden was gradual for one or two reasons. I wasn't sure what would grow, so in the beginning it was a big adventure, planting what I thought should grow and in many cases did not. I also purchased books on woodland and shade loving plants and sought advice from people who know about such things.

As the trees grew, parts of the garden were quite dry and other parts exceedingly wet. The garden would be at least 2 metres below the Magheratimpany Road, and there are field drains coming onto our land from the fields on the other side of the road. We have used these field drains to our advantage by opening them up to water the garden.

A year ago, the winter project for my husband was to take all the lower branches off the trees in the shelter belt, also to clear the ivy that was growing up all the trees. We have noticed over the years that any conifers festooned in ivy are very vulnerable to gale damage. The area that had been cleared was soon discovered to be very dry and even rainfall did not penetrate the ground. On the north side of the garden we have a 'sheugh' which has water running only when there is heavy rain. After the first downpours we had in July 2007, my husband got out his mattock and made what we laughingly call a 'levada', not quite so impressive as the ones we had seen while holidaying in Santana on the island of Madeira, and released the water from the 'sheugh'. Gradually over two hours the whole garden was flooded and well watered, a slate was placed across the head of the 'levada' to stop any more water coming into the main part of the garden.

It was now possible to dig the ground and prepare the soil for planting, before the soil was not dissimilar to concrete, and worms were not to be found.

Dactylorhiza

With the ivy growing on the ground, I used an old lawnmower, lifted the blades very high off the ground, just in case there were stones amongst it, and mowed the ivy as one does with grass. By mowing the ivy, a method which seems to have worked, the growth of the ivy on the ground has slowed.

In a woodland garden, you are never going to have bright colours. Instead there will be restful subtle shades of green. This does not mean the garden will not be exciting; there are so many plants to suit this situation. Once the snowdrops have finished flowering, the trilliums will be coming into flower, along with meconopsis and primula, hosta, hardy orchids. I find brunnera useful, there are many varieties around now well worth a place in any garden, starting to flower very early in the year, first the pretty blue forget-me-not flower followed by the wonderful metallic leaves. *Saxifrage fortunei*, is autumn flowering; the leaves are very glossy, and usually red underneath, depending on the variety. It makes a useful edging plant along the pathways around the garden, I would also use Hosta plants in the same way, and most Hosta do better out of direct sun and can tolerate dry ground. Dry ground, no slugs.

When we think of woodland, the first plant comes to mind is a fern, and there are so many to choose from, but *Dicksonia antarctica* and *D. fibrosa*, tree ferns I feel give a bit of glamour to the garden and I would not be without any of the tree ferns.

Depending on the size of your garden many of the *Euphorbia* grows well in shade, some do outstay their welcome; so if the garden is small, do not plant *Euphorbia griffithii* 'Dixter'. This plant is colourful and as the most glorious autumn colour, but it does run.

Here are a few plants I could not be without in the Woodland Garden:
Anemone nemorosa
Arisaema sp.
Cacalia delphiniifolia
Cardamine dentaria
Cardiocrinum cathayanum
Cardiocrinum giganteum v. yunnanense
Cypripedium sp.
Dactylorhiza elata, D. foliosa, D. fuchsii
Disporum cantoniense
Disporum flavum
Disporum maculatum
Disporum pernyi
Disporum smithii
Epimedium sp.
Erythronium sp.
Fritillaria sp.
Galanthus sp.

Helleborus sp.
Hosta sp.
Lilium mackliniae
Meconopsis betonicifolia, M. grandis. M. napaulensis, M. paniculata
Paris any
Podophyllum delavayii; P.difforme
Saxifraga fortunei
Shortia uniflora
Smilacina sp.
Syneilesis aconitifolia
Trillium sp.

Acknowledgements:
Marie Davis (Irish spelling): *sheugh*

The Way That We Went!

*A retracing of some of the footsteps
of Robert Lloyd Praeger*
by Jim Dennison

For those familiar with the history of Irish Botany, R. L. Praeger will need no introduction. However, for readers not familiar with him or his work, some background information on this most remarkable and indomitable of men is required.

Robert Lloyd Praeger was born in 1865 in County Down, the son of a Dutch linen merchant and an Irish mother and in spite of the fact that he did not study botany professionally (he took an engineering degree at Queens University in Belfast) his contribution to the recording of Irish Flora over a fifty year period is, without doubt, one of the most singularly important contributions to the field. The Reverend Caleb Threlkeld's 'Synopsis Stirpium Hibernicarum', published in 1726 was the first serious attempt to catalogue Irish flora although this was mainly confined to Dublin and its hinterland. Praeger's 'Irish Topographical Botany' published by the Royal Irish Academy in 1901 was therefore a landmark work in the history of Irish Botany as a whole and was considered as a companion to the two editions of 'Cybele Hibernica' first published in 1866 by D. Moore and A.G.More and revised in 1898 by N.Colgan and R.Scully, and giving for the first time a detailed geographical analysis of

Polypodium cambricum var semilacerum

Ireland's vascular flora. It was undertaken in just five years and in the preface to the work Praeger noted that the need for an 'Irish Topographical Botany' was forcibly brought to his mind in 1895 when, in perusing a copy of the

'London Catalogue of British Plants' he noticed that Ireland was excluded from the census, owing to the absence of detailed information concerning the distribution of plants on the island. In fact Ireland was placed on the same footing as the Channel Islands – its existence only being recognized when a plant occurred in Ireland, but not in Great Britain.

Praeger, following on from the recommendations of C.C.Babbington in 1859, divided Ireland into 40 vice counties in 1901 which correspond in the main with the Irish counties, but with the larger ones sub-divided to make the task easier, and set about systematically collecting data on each one. Fortunately the more remote parts of the country, Cork, Kerry, Donegal, Derry and Antrim were counties where the flora's were in the process of being recorded or had being covered by amongst others, Colgan, Scully, and Hart, not that this deterred Praeger from visiting them. He acquired an intimate knowledge of Ireland by walking in excess of 6500 kilometres to collect data. He considered a normal days field work as" twelve hours spent covering 20-25 miles with a minimum of 15 and a maximum of 35". Each county had to be systematically covered so that neither plants of early spring, summer or autumn should escape his notice.

He was a prolific writer, publishing papers on Sedum and Sempervivum amongst a host of other horticultural articles. His books, apart from the 'Irish Topographical Botany',, included 'A Tourists Flora of the West of Ireland in 1909, 'The Botanist in Ireland' in 1934. In 1937 he published his best known work, "The Way That I Went' ..'an Irishman in Ireland" a wonderfully poetic and personal account of his travels throughout Ireland, not only recording flora, but the geology and also the antiquities of each county.

I began this article by referring to him as indomitable. Well – his descriptions of some of the difficulties he encountered whilst out in the field give ample testimony to his spirit. He notes for instance that it is a matter of regret that the climate makes it so uncomfortable to get wet in and so difficult to get dry.

'The clothes that the prevailing temperature compels us to wear, (tweeds) are even, in summer, of a thickness which renders them capable of absorbing a great amount of water, and the air is of a dampness which slows up evaporation, and so keeps them wet'. He was referring here to the fact that when he had to cross streams too deep for wading he had for a while carried a rubber bag into which he could put his clothes and tow them across behind him whilst he swam. Eventually he decided that this wasn't worth the effort and simply swam across fully clothed, slowly drying out over the next few days. He did though wear a pair of boots with holes in the soles so that water would drain through! That pretty well fits the description of indomitable for me.

In June 2007, the eightieth anniversary of the publication of 'The Way that I went', Martin Rickard, one of the leading authorities on hardy ferns, and I decided to pay our own particular homage to R.L Praeger by re-visiting some of the locations where he originally recorded some of Ireland's rarest ferns.

Now Martin and I don't do indomitability (at least I don't) so, suitably attired and with no holes in our shoes, we set out for South East Mayo where Praeger noted the only recorded Irish station for the Limestone Oak fern, *Gymnocarpium robertianum*. According to the 'Census Catalogue of Vascular Plants in Ireland', Scannell and Synott 1987. this plant was recorded as being located in two Irish stations, one in East Mayo and the other in County Louth). However, the species distribution maps of the Botanical Society of Britain and Ireland for 2000 onwards only record the one site in East Mayo. Praeger writes of its location being, 'just three miles north west of Headford on a low rocky limestone outcrop'. He also noted that Ireland is a wide and lonely country and 'if you want to see how lonely it can be, take the new road from Galway to Headford. After a couple of miles the hummocky limestone ground disappears and you enter a stretch of road dead level, dead straight, with neither hedges nor houses' ... the first time I traversed that heartbreaking thoroughfare, the land was wrapped in a wet mist driving before a wind that moaned ... and so for a mile and a half I walked alone thinking of death,' save that the mile and a half turned out to be six!

Of course the landscape has changed since Praeger's visit, with hedgerows and farms, and the odd bungalow dotted over the landscape, and thankfully there was no moaning wind to remind Martin and me of our mortality. We drove to Headford and through it onto the only road running in a northwesterly direction until we had traveled roughly two to three miles when we began searching for rocky outcrops. Being initially unsuccessful we were about to retrace our steps and drove into a narrow lane to reverse the car when we spotted to our left about three hundred metres in the distance on a low hill, our first rocky outcrop, or to be more precise, a small section of limestone pavement. When Praeger traversed the country nearly a century ago, he remarked that 'Ireland is a delightful country for the pursuit of work in the field. Enclosed or preserved ground is seldom met with, and the country is free and open…' How times change. Now

Gymnacarpium robrtianum

on foot we crossed a farmyard, and a small field and over a fence onto the outcrop. Here there were alpine plants normally associated with the famous limestone pavement of the Burren. Orchids such as *Orchis mascula* , the early spring orchid, both purple and white forms, *Geranium sanguineum,* bloody cranesbill, *Geranium robertianum,* the common dog violet, *Viola riviana,*

Helianthemum canum, the hoary rockrose, saxifages, to name but a few and then
Asplenium Scolopendrium, Asplenium trichomanies subsp. *quadrivalens, Asplenium
ruta muraria, Cystopteris fragilis, Dryopteris affinis, Dryopteris dilitata, Polystichum
setiferum, Pteridium aquilinum,* but no Oak fern. Then after twenty minutes or so
scouring the outcrop, a yelp from Martin and there it was - three or four small
clumps waving in the breeze. The only recorded Irish station still hanging in
there. It differs from *Gymnocarpium dryopteris* the Woodland oak fern which
is locally present in Ireland but mainly in the north east of the country by its
much paler less vivid green colour and of course from the fact that while *G.
robertianum* is a calcicole, *G. dryopteris* likes acidic conditions.

That victory being then accomplished, we then motored on to Sligo
where we overnighted before beginning our search for another one of Praeger's
listings, and one of the few Irish locations for the Holly fern, *Polystichum lonchitis.*

Dartry Mountains, Co. Sligo

Driving north east out of Sligo Town, along the shores of Lough Gill, we now
entered County Leitrim and followed the R288 up to through the Glencar
valley towards Glenade, with the Dartry mountains, of which Benbulben's

spectacular plateau forms the western extremity, to the north of us.

The range is made of limestone capped in parts with Yoredale rock, a particular form of limestone, and is just over 2000ft at its highest point. We chose a starting point approximately half way along the valley and began a steep climb up to the base of the north east facing cliff face, and there began our search with a couple of Perigrine falcons for company with their strident tcha-tcha-tcha's echoing from the cliffs - angry at being disturbed. *Aslenium viride* was fairly well distributed here, in one of it's very few Irish stations, with *Aslenium trichomanes* subsp. *quadrivalens, Asplenium ruta muraria, Asplenium scolopendrium, Dryopteris aemula, Dryopteris affinis, Dryopteris dilitata, Polypodium vulgare, Polypodium intejrectum,* and one clump of *Polypodium cambrium. Polystichum setiferum,* the ubiquitous *Pteridilum aqualinum* and again *Cystopteris fragilis.* Also a number of Equisitums, *E. arvense, E. sylvaticum, and E. telemateia.*

Very quickly the principal object of our search, *Polystichum lonchitis* the holly fern, which is a montane fern only growing above 1000ft. came into view in some of the many fissures marking the cliff face. Although *P. lonchitis* can grow to a length in excess of 30 centimetres none of the plants we found approached this size. The only other two stations for this fern are in the mountains of north west Donegal and Connemara.

Having then completed the days main task we then awarded ourselves enough bonus points to last a summer when, in a deep fissure, Martin spotted what at first appeared to be the young fronds of *Polystichum aculeatum* but on examination on site and later, we now believe to be *Polystichum* × *lonchitiforme* the hybrid of *Polystichum setiferum* and *Polystichum lonchitis.* This plant was first recorded in this locale in the mid —seventies (on broken limestone scree in an open habitat not in the rock face however) and is the only recorded station in Britain and Ireland. In fact it is only in Greece apparently that a single plant was also recorded. "Its rarity springs from the fact that the two parent species are normally altitudinally separate through most of their ranges. *P setiferum* being mainly a southern and lowland plant. *P. lonchitis* mainly a northern alpine. Only along the extreme atlantic coasts can alpines normally descend to near sea level because of cool summers and southern plants spread north because of mild winters, producing conditions where both species can meet". It looks remarkably similar to *Polystichum × illyricum,* also recorded from here, and also the only Irish station. We were dissuaded of any possible confusion nevertheless as one of the parents of *P. illyricum, Polystichum aculeatum* was absent from the locality. To add some weight to our conviction, the spores on examination appeared to be abortive although this is also the case with *P. illyricum.*

Feeling pretty well sated with these successes, we then began our downward climb only to stumble across what at first appeared to be *Dryopteris expansa.* If so, this was the first recorded siting of the species in Ireland. Since we returned home however, Christopher Fraser Jenkins, who would be considered the world's leading authority on Dryopteris species, was sent a photograph of the plant. He tentatively believes it to be an odd form of *Dryopteris dilitata.* Further investigation, possibly in the form of a chromosome count would help to eliminate any uncertainty although I am told by botanists at Trinity College Dublin that the group is particularly difficult to identify, particularly if the chromosomes are small. Could it be *Dryopteris × ambroseae?* The hybrid between *D. dilitata* and *D. expansa.* Although *D. expansa* has not been recorded from Ireland, *Dryopteris × remota* whose parents are *D. affinis subsp. affinis* **and** *D. expansa* has been recorded in two stations, one in North Kerry and the other in South East Galway?

In August 2008 we paid a return visit to the above sites to photograph the plants at the end of the season and also to collect a specimen of the *Dryopteris expansa* for a chromosome count. This we did, but then undertook a search along the shores of Lough Gill where last year we had seen the shriveled remains of the scarcest of the Polypodiums. *Polypodium cambricum,* the Southern Polypody. This Polypody produces new fronds in August/September and is wintergreen through to the following spring. It is also the polypody from which the largest number of varieties and forms have formed.

To our amazement and delight we found not only the type plant in abundance in what surely must be one of the largest stations of this species on the island, with frond lengths approaching 60cm, but also found *P. cambricum* var. semilacerum and a very attractive, serrated form. In addition, on the southern side of the lake we found all three varieties of Polypody growing adjacent to each other. *P. vulgare, P. interjectum and P. cambricum*

This is most unusual, frequently one might find two of the species close together but not three. The significance of this was not lost on us as we then may have found two hybrids. *Polypodium shivasia* whose parents are *P. interjectum* and *P. cambricum* and then *Polypodium font –queri* whose parents are *P. vulgare* and *P. cambricum*. Both of these hybrids are extremely rare in Britain and Ireland. Only one other station for *P. font-queri* being recorded in Ireland in County Kerry.

Asplenium onopteris

On our return to Limerick to complete our fern botanizing, we visited Foynes to check out a Polypodium that I had seen in the winter and that might be something interesting. It turned out not to be anything extraordinary, but on our return to our car we did encounter what may turn out to be a very special fern that is also extremely rare and one that was last recorded from Foynes in 1906 in '*The Flora of the Barony of Shanid*' This is *Asplenium onopteris* the Irish Spleenwort, recorded only from two or three other sites in West Cork and Waterford, and completely absent from Britain. At the time of writing this is awaiting confirmation. The only possible confusion would be with a very luxuriant form of *Asplenium adiantum-nigrum*? Who knows – with the wet summer we have just had, anything is possible!

The majority of this article was first published in the 'Pteridologist' in February 2008.

References:
N.Colgan and R.W.Scully 'Cybele Hibernica' 2nd.ed. 1898
T.G Curtis and H.N.McGough, 'The Irish Red Data Book' 1980
H.C Hart. 'Flora of Donegal' 1898.
C.H.Nelson R.L Praeger. 'Bibliographic addenda and enendata' 1998
E.Newman 'A History of British Ferns' 1844
C.N.Page 'The Ferns of Britain and Ireland'. 1982
R.L.Praeger 'Irish Topographical Botany' 1901
R.L.Prager 'The Way That I Went', 1937
M.J.Scannell and D.M Synott, 'Census Catalogue of the Flora of Ireland.' OPW.1989
Distribution Maps – Botanical Society of Britain and Ireland